DIY
DESIGN *and* REMODEL
Like a *Pro*

Unleash Your Inner Designer

TAM NGUYEN

COPYRIGHT

DIY Design & Remodel Like a Pro
Unleash Your Inner Designer
© 2025 Tam Nguyen
All rights reserved. No part of this publication may be reproduced, distributed, or transmitted in any form or by any means, including photocopying, recording, or other electronic or mechanical methods, without the prior written permission of the author, except in the case of brief quotations embodied in critical reviews and certain other noncommercial uses permitted by copyright law. First Edition: Fall 2025
ISBN: 979-8-9985848-1-7
Published by Quantum Burst Publishing LLC
7901 4th Street N #300
St. Petersburg, FL 33702
Interior Design: Tam Nguyen
Cover Design: A. Cheakinah
Photography: Tam Nguyen
Author Contact: Tam Nguyen
Email: tam@tam-interiors.com

DISCLAIMER

The information in this book is based on the author's experience and knowledge at the time of writing. While every effort has been made to ensure accuracy and thoroughness, the author and publisher assume no responsibility for errors, omissions, or contrary interpretations of the subject matter herein. The reader assumes responsibility for using the information provided.

Printed in the United States of America.

DEDICATION

First and foremost, thank God for blessings and graces.

To my mother, whose courage to send her twelve-year-old daughter alone on a boat to seek freedom planted the seeds of endless possibilities. Your sacrifice gave me the greatest
gift of all—the opportunity to dream, fail, succeed, and live freely in this great nation.

To America, the land of opportunity, which welcomed a young refugee and provided the foundation for all my achievements. Your promise of freedom and possibility has shaped every aspect of my journey.

To my son, who has watched me reinvent myself multiple times, never settling for less than what brings joy to my heart. May you always have the courage to follow your dreams and the wisdom to know that it's never too late to begin again.

To all aspiring designers and homeowners who dream of creating beautiful, purposeful spaces, may this book serve as your trusted guide and inspiration. Remember that great design is not about perfection but about creating spaces that enhance lives and bring joy to
those who inhabit them.

To all those who dare to dream of new beginnings: may you find the courage to take that first step, knowing that every journey begins with a single moment of brave decision.

Finally, I thank myself for not giving up.

DIY Design and Remodel Like A Pro

Unleash Your Inner Designer

Image Credits:

This book contains professional photographs from the author's personal project portfolio and AI-generated images explicitly created for this publication.

Professional photographs are copyright © 2025 Tam Nguyen.

AI-generated photos are made using AI ChatGPT, and Midjourney was used under appropriate licensing agreements. All rights reserved.

The information presented in this book reflects the author's professional experience and knowledge at the time of publication. While every effort has been made to ensure accuracy and thoroughness, the author and publisher make no representations or warranties regarding the accuracy or completeness of the contents and expressly disclaim any implied warranties. The advice and strategies contained herein may not be suitable for every situation. Readers should consult with appropriate professionals where applicable.

Business corporations, service marks, and trade names referenced in this book are the property of their respective owners and are used only for identification and explanation without intent to infringe. No part of this publication may be reproduced, stored in a retrieval system, or transmitted in any form or by any means, electronic, mechanical, photocopying, recording, scanning, or otherwise, except as permitted under Section 107 or 108 of the 1976 United States Copyright Act, without either the prior written permission of the publisher or author.

International Rights:
For information on international rights and translation, please get in touch with Totam Publishing LLC at the address above.

Digital Rights:
This copyrighted work's unauthorized reproduction or distribution in any digital format is illegal. No part of this book may be reproduced, scanned, or distributed electronically without written permission.

Trademarks:
Product or corporate names may be trademarks or registered trademarks and are used only for identification and explanation without intent to infringe.

Limit of Liability/Disclaimer of Warranty:

While the publisher and author have used their best efforts in preparing this book, they make no representations or warranties concerning the accuracy or completeness of the contents and expressly disclaim any implied warranties. The advice and strategies contained herein may not be suitable for your situation. You should consult with a professional where appropriate. Neither the publisher nor the author shall be liable for any loss of profit or Other commercial damages, including but not limited to special, incidental, consequential, or other damages.

Library Cataloging Publication Data:

Nguyen, Tam

DIY Design Remodel Like a Pro, Unleash Your Inner Designer / Tam Nguyen p. cm.

Includes bibliographical references and index.

ISBN: 979-89985848-0-0

Printed in the United States of America 10 9 8 7 6 5 4 3 2 1

First Edition

Permission RequestGuidelines

To request permission for the usage of content from this book, please submit a detailed request including:

Contact Information: Published by Quantum Burst Publishing LLC

7901 4th Street N #300

St. Petersburg, FL 33702

Email: tam@tam-interiors.com

Digital Rights and Usage Guidelines

Digital Format Specifications

This work is available in the following authorized digital formats:

- eBook (ePub)
- Enhanced PDF
- Interactive Digital Edition
- Print Edition

Each format contains unique digital watermarking and tracking features to protect against unauthorized reproduction. Digital editions are personalized to the original purchaser and may not be transferred or shared without explicit permission from the publisher.

Required Information for Requests

1. Specific content to be used(page numbers, sections, images)
2. Intended use and format
3. Distribution scope
4. The time frame for usage
5. Contact information for follow-up Response time: 10-15 business days

International Rights Information

International publishing rights are managed directly by Quantum Burst Publishing LLC. For inquiries regarding:

- Translation rights
- International distribution
- Territory-specific licensing
- Foreign language editions
- International adaptations

Please get in touch with our rights department at tam@tam-interiors.com

Image Usage Guidelines

This publication contains two categories of images:

- Professional Project Photography
- Copyright © 2025 Tam Nguyen
- All rights reserved
- Usage requires explicit written permission
- Attribution required for authorized use
- High-resolution files available for licensed usage

Extended Trademark Notice

Product names, brands, and other trademarks referenced in this book are the property of their respective trademark holders. These references are made for instructional purposes only. No endorsement is implied nor should be inferred. The use of third-party trademarks does not indicate any relationship, sponsorship, or endorsement between Quantum Burst Publishing LLC and the owners of these trademarks.

Liability Limitation Extension

The information provided in this book, including but not limited to text, images, specifications, and recommendations, is for general informational purposes only. While the author and publisher have made every effort to ensure the accuracy and completeness of this, They cannot and do not guarantee that the information is accurate, complete, reliable, current, or error-free.

AI-Generated Imagery

- Created using AI ChatGPT and Midjourney
- Licensed for use in this publication
- May not be extracted or repurposed
- Subject to platform terms of service
- Identified within the text

SPECIFIC DISCLAIMER

1. Construction and Renovation Advice

- Local building codes may vary
- Professional consultation recommended
- Permits may be required
- Safety considerations paramount
- Insurance requirements vary

2. Design Recommendations

- Results may vary
- Professional assistance advised
- Cost estimates approximate
- Material availability varies
- Regional differences apply

3. Product Recommendations

- Availability subject to change
- Prices may vary
- Specifications may change
- Regional variations exist
- Performance may vary

USAGE GUIDELINES FOR EDUCATIONAL SETTINGS

This work may be used in educational settings under the following conditions:

Academic Use

- Limited excerpt reproduction allowed
- Attribution required
- Not for commercial use
- Class size restrictions apply
- Time limitations enforced

Digital Platform Integration

For integration with digital platforms, including but not limited to:

- Learning Management Systems
- Digital Libraries
- Content Management Systems
- Online Course Platforms
- Mobile Applications

Please get in touch with Quantum Burst Publishing LLC for licensing information and technical specifications.

Training Programs

- License required for systematic use
- Student number limitations
- Materials reproduction restricted
- Attribution mandatory
- Usage reporting required

Professional Organization Usage

Professional organizations wishing to utilize content for:

- Training Programs
- Certification Courses
- Professional Development
- Member Resources
- Industry Education

Must obtain specific licensing agreements through Quantum Burst Publishing LLC.

Enhanced Digital Rights Information

Digital publication and distribution of this work are protected under multiple frameworks to ensure content integrity and authorized usage. The following specifications apply to all digital versions of this work:

Digital Format Protection

This work employs multiple layers of digital protection: Digital Rights Management (DRM) Systems:All electronic versions utilize industry-standard DRM protection to prevent unauthorized copying or sharing. Each authorized copy contains unique identifiers linking it to the original purchaser.

Access Authorization:

Digital editions require authenticated access through approved platformsand devices. Multi-device access is limited to prevent unauthorized distribution while maintaining convenience for legitimate users.

Content Protection:

All digital editions incorporate watermarking and tracking technology. These features ensure content integrity while allowing legitimate use across authorized devices and platforms.

INTERNATIONAL COPYRIGHT PROTECTION

The Berne Convention:

Protection extends automatically to all signatory countries (179 member states) without the requirement of formal registration.

WIPO Copyright Treaty:

Digital rights protection extends across international borders, specifically addressing electronic and internet distribution.

Regional Protections:

European Union: Protected under the EU Copyright Directive.
Asia Pacific: Protected under various regional copyright agreements
Americas: Protected under Pan-American Copyright Conventions

Translation Rights:

Quantum Burst Publishing LLC exclusively manages all translation rights. Unauthorized translations in any format or medium are strictly prohibited.

CONTENT

COPYRIGHT	iii
DISCLAIMER	v
DEDICATION	vii
INTRODUCTION	xv
Chapter 1: Understanding Purpose-Driven Design	1
Chapter 2: Assessing Your Space and Needs	5
Chapter 3: Design Styles with Purpose	9
Chapter 4: Planning Your Purpose-Driven Project	29
Chapter 5: Budgeting with Purpose	33
Chapter 6: Working with Professionals	43
Chapter 7: Managing Your Renovation Project	49
Chapter 8: Smart Home Integration	51
Chapter 9: Material Selection and Implementation	59
Chapter 10: Lighting Design for Purpose	61
Chapter 11: Smart Home Technology Integration	65
Chapter 12: Sustainable Energy Systems	67
Chapter 13: Creating Healthy Indoor Environments	73
Chapter 14: Purpose-Driven Storage Solutions	75
Chapter 15: Future-Proofing Your Home	79
Chapter 16: Curated Shopping Resources	87
Chapter 17: Interior Design and Renovation Mentorship Program	97
Enrollment Information	100

INTRODUCTION

Life often takes us down unexpected paths, each offering valuable lessons that shape who we become. My journey began in 1980 when, at just twelve years old, my mother sent me on a small boat with 49 strangers, fleeing Vietnam after the war. That frightened young refugee could never have imagined the road ahead—a path that would lead through the restaurant industry, college classrooms, and ultimately to a fulfilling career in interior design and construction project management.

With its boundless opportunities, America became more than just a refuge; it became the canvas upon which I could paint my dreams. As a teenager, I initially aspired to be a fashion designer, but life had other plans. I took a practical route, majoring in accounting and building a successful career operating two Asian restaurants in Southern California. Yet after eight years in the restaurant business, my persistent creative spark led me back to school, where I earned a bachelor's degree in Interior Design from the Art Institute of Fort Lauderdale, Florida.

This decision began a sixteen-year journey in interior design and construction project management. Over the years, I've had the privilege of helping countless clients transform their spaces into beautifully designed environments that reflect their lifestyles and aspirations. Each project has reinforced my belief in the power of thoughtful design, the intersection of aesthetics, functionality, and personal expression.

As I prepare to close this chapter of my professional life and step into the unknown again, I want to share the knowledge and insights I've gained. This Book is more than just a guide to home renovation; it embodies the lessons learned from countless projects, challenges overcome, and dreams realized.

While interior design encompasses hundreds of styles from the early 1900s, I've focused on seven styles that best serve modern living. As a minimalist, I value purposeful selection, and these styles strike the perfect balance of aesthetics, functionality, and adaptability for contemporary homes.

This Book will walk you through every stage of the renovation process, from selecting a design style that resonates with your lifestyle to creating mood boards, setting realistic budgets, choosing the right professionals, and managing your project to completion. By sharing my expertise, I hope to empower you to take control of your renovation journey while saving significantly on design fees, savings that can be redirected toward quality materials, better appliances, or other improvements that will enhance your daily life. Each chapter builds upon the previous one, creating a step-by-step roadmap for your renovation project. I've included the what and how of design, renovation, and the why helping you understand the reasoning behind each decision. This knowledge will enable you to make informed choices that serve your immediate needs and long-term goals.

Throughout my career, I've believed that good design should be accessible to everyone. While professional design services can be costly, the principles and practices of great design shouldn't be reserved for those who can afford high fees. This Book aims to democratize design knowledge, directly putting professional insights and strategies into your hands.

As you embark on your renovation journey, remember that every space has potential, and every challenge has a solution. While this Book marks the end of my chapter in professional design, it opens a new chapter for you, one where you can confidently create the home you've always envisioned.

I remain deeply grateful to this country for the opportunities it has provided me. I am honored to give back by sharing my knowledge with you.

If you need guidance during your renovation journey, you'll find my contact information at the end of this Book. I welcome your questions and look forward to hearing about your success stories.
May your renovation journey be rewarding, and may your transformed space bring you joy for years.With gratitude and optimism,

Tam Nguyen

CHAPTER 01

UNDERSTANDING PURPOSE-DRIVEN DESIGN

In today's world of endless design inspiration and instant gratification, it's easy to lose sight of what truly matters in home design. After sixteen years as an interior designer and project manager, I've learned that the most successful homes aren't necessarily the largest or most expensively furnished. Instead, they are the ones that genuinely support and enhance the lives of those who live in them.

What is Purpose-Driven Design?
The purpose-driven design represents a fundamental shift from traditional home design and renovation approaches. Instead of beginning with aesthetic preferences or current trends, this method starts with a deep understanding of how you live and what you truly need from your space. Every design decision is made with function in mind, ensuring that the result adds real value to your daily life.

The Difference Between Aesthetic and Purpose-Driven Design Consider the difference between a purely aesthetic approach and purpose-driven design. Traditional design might focus on creating a stunning kitchen that looks perfect in photos but doesn't meet the functional needs of the homeowner. Conversely, purpose-driven design ensures that your kitchen is visually appealing, supports your cooking style, accommodates your storage needs, and facilitates comfortable interaction with family and friends.

THE KEY PRINCIPLES OF PURPOSE-DRIVEN DESIGN

The key principles of purpose-driven design include:

Functional Priority

Prioritizing function means considering how spaces will be used before making decisions about appearance. This doesn't mean sacrificing beauty but allowing beauty to emerge naturally from thoughtful functionality.

Efficient Use of Space

Bigger isn't always better. A well-designed, smaller space can often serve its purpose more effectively than a larger one that lacks thoughtful planning. Efficiency also includes energy use, maintenance, and long-term adaptability, extending beyond square footage.

Sustainable Thinking

Sustainability goes beyond eco-friendly materials. It encompasses choosing durable materials, implementing energy-efficient systems, and creating flexible, evolving spaces. This principle is about minimizing waste in terms of resources and space and designing homes that maintain their value and functionality in the long run.

The Pitfalls of Real Estate Trends

Real estate trends have often prioritized size over functionality, resulting in homes with impressive square footage that may lack proper space utilization. Purpose-driven design challenges this notion by creating spaces that truly serve their inhabitants, minimizing waste, and ensuring spaces are functional, efficient, and sustainable.

Understanding How You Live

Understanding your daily patterns is the foundation of purpose-driven design. Before making any design decisions, observe how you currently use your space. Take note of where you naturally gather, which areas feel welcoming, and where you face frustrations. These observations provide valuable insights into what's working and what isn't in your current environment.

Adapting to Changing Needs

Consider how your space requirements change throughout the day and across seasons. A purpose-driven home accommodates these variations efficiently, perhaps through flexible spaces that serve multiple functions or smart storage solutions that allow easy transitions between different uses.

Integrating Technology for Functionality

Technology integration in purpose-driven design focuses on practical utility rather than novelty. Smart home features should simplify daily routines and enhance comfort, all while remaining intuitive. For example, automated lighting that supports natural circadian rhythms or climate control systems that learn your preferences to optimize comfort and energy efficiency can be powerful additions to a purpose-driven home.

Planning for the Future

Implementing purpose-driven design requires careful planning and may challenge conventional wisdom about home design. For instance, it might mean allocating more space to frequently used areas while reducing the size of rarely used formal spaces. It might also involve investing in high-quality materials for high-wear areas while opting for more modest choices in less critical spaces.

Long-Term Value and Adaptability

The purpose-driven design also emphasizes long-term value and adaptability. As your needs evolve, your home should be able to adapt without requiring major renovations. This might involve creating flexible spaces for different purposes or ensuring that your infrastructure supports future technology needs.

Sustainability and Satisfaction

Prioritizing purpose first often results in more sustainable and satisfying homes. When spaces function well, we're less likely to feel the need for frequent updates or renovations, reducing both environmental impact and long-term costs. Sustainability goes beyond material choices and extends to how spaces are used and maintained, ensuring a home that stands the test of time.

CHAPTER 02

ASSESSING YOUR SPACE AND NEEDS

B efore embarking on any design project, a thorough assessment of your current space and needs provides the foundation for successful outcomes. Professional designers approach this evaluation.
Systematically, considering both the physical characteristics of a space and the human factors that influence how spaces function. Understanding your space begins with documenting existing conditions. This goes beyond basic measurements to include an analysis of natural light patterns, airflow, sound transmission, and traffic flow. These factors significantly impact how comfortable and functional a space feels, yet they're often overlooked in basic renovations.

Natural Light Analysis

Observe how sunlight moves through your space throughout the day and across seasons. Track where and when direct sunlight enters different rooms, noting its beneficial effects and potential issues like glare or heat gain. This information will influence decisions about window treatments, furniture placement, and potential architectural modifications.

Traffic Flow Analysis

Examine how people naturally move through spaces. Observe congestion points, preferred pathways, and areas that collect clutter. These patterns often reveal where current layouts fail to support natural movement or where storage solutions might be needed.

Sound Transmission

Notice how noise travels between spaces

and where acoustic issues create discomfort. Understanding these patterns helps inform insulation, door placement, and material selection decisions.

Infrastructure Assessment

Evaluate the systems that support daily life in your home. This includes electrical capacity, plumbing systems, HVAC performance, and technological infrastructure. Understanding these systems' current capabilities and limitations helps plan improvements that align with immediate needs and future possibilities.

Assessing How You Use Your Space

Beyond physical characteristics, understanding how you use your space provides crucial insights. Keep a detailed activity log for at least a week, noting:

When and how different are used

- Storage needs and current limitations
- Furniture arrangements and their effectiveness
- Lighting requirements for different activities
- Temperature and comfort patterns throughout the day
- Pay particular attention to pain points in your current space.

These might include insufficient storage, poor lighting, uncomfortable temperature variations, or awkward traffic patterns. Often, these frustrations indicate opportunities for improvement through thoughtful design.

Consider Both Current and Future Needs

Consider how your space requirements may change over the next five to ten years. Consider factors like:

Family composition changes

- Aging-place requirements
- Work-from-home needs
- Entertainment preferences

Storage requirements

- Technology integration
- Seasonal variations also impact space requirements. Consider how your needs change throughout the year, including:

Storage for seasonal items

- Indoor-outdoor connections
- Natural light preferences
- Temperature control requirements
- Changes in activity patterns

Document everything thoroughly using photographs, measurements, and detailed notes. This documentation becomes a valuable reference during the design process and helps ensure no important considerations are overlooked.

External Factors and Constraints

The professional assessment also includes an evaluation of local climate considerations and how they affect your home's performance. Understanding weather patterns, solar exposure, and seasonal variations helps inform decisions about insulation, window specifications, and HVAC requirements. Finally, assess your project's constraints, including:

- Budget limitations

- Timeline requirements
- Local building codes
- Structural limitations
- Historic preservation requirements
- Neighbourhood guidelines

This comprehensive assessment provides the foundation for purpose-driven design decisions that truly serve your needs while respecting project constraints.

CHAPTER

03

DESIGN STYLES WITH PURPOSE

Understanding design styles through the lens of functionality allows us to make choices that enhance our daily lives while creating aesthetically pleasing environments. Rather than merely following trends, the purpose-driven design focuses on how different styles can support specific lifestyle needs and preferences. Modern design styles have evolved to address contemporary living requirements while maintaining distinct characteristics that serve particular purposes. We will explore seven key styles that support modern lifestyles and offer timeless appeal: **Modernism, Modern Industrial, Modern Ranch, Scandinavian, Cosmopolitan**

DESIGN STYLES

Modernism

It emphasizes clean lines and functional beauty, making it ideal for those who value efficiency and organized living. Rooted in the principle that form should follow function, modernist spaces are designed with every element serving a clear purpose. For example, a modernist kitchen might feature smooth cabinet fronts without hardware, creating visual calm and simplifying cleaning and maintenance. The style's emphasis on natural light and open spaces promotes well-being while reducing energy consumption.

Modern Industrial style

This style celebrates the raw beauty of architecture.

Hidden elements create honest, functional spaces that easily adapt to changing needs. This style is particularly effective in urban environments or renovated spaces, where existing structural features can become design highlights. For instance, exposed ductwork adds visual interest and simplifies maintenance, and future modifications. The use of durable materials and flexible spaces supports long-term sustainability.

Modern Ranch

Brings contemporary comfort to traditional Ranch homes, focusing on indoor-outdoor connectivity and accessible living. This style is especially suitable for those who value seamless integration between interior and exterior spaces while ensuring single-level accessibility. Large windows and sliding doors provide visual connections to nature and support natural ventilation and passive solar benefits when oriented correctly.

Scandinavian design

Embodies the idea that beauty and function are Inseparable. Known for creating bright, practical spaces that are both minimal and warm, this style features light woods, natural materials, and thoughtful storage solutions, making it ideal for those seeking organized, comfortable environments. Scandinavian design promotes psychological well-being and practical living by emphasizing natural light and low-maintenance materials.

The Cosmopolitan design

This design reflects a sophisticated urban lifestyle. It is characterized by an eclectic mix of global influences, contemporary luxury, and a focus on entertainment-friendly spaces. This style is ideal for professional couples or city dwellers who embrace bold colors, clean lines, and statement pieces while ensuring functional social gatherings and relaxation spaces. The Cosmopolitan style creates a refined yet welcoming atmosphere for modern living.

Minimalism

This style is rooted in the idea that "less is more." This design style prioritizes simplicity and decluttered spaces, focusing on the essentials and removing unnecessary elements. It's especially suitable for those who thrive in clean, serene environments. By emphasizing negative space and carefully selecting functional furnishings, minimalism enhances a room's visual clarity and functionality.

Modern Zen

This style merges the Eastern philosophies of simplicity and tranquillity with contemporary design principles. It creates calm, serene spaces that promote mindfulness and optimal relaxation. Elements like neutral colors, natural textures, and the use of space for meditation or reflection are key. Modern Zen spaces are intentionally designed to support a balanced and peaceful lifestyle.

When selecting a design style, it's essential to consider how it aligns with your daily routines and long-term goals. For example, a young family may find Scandinavian design's durability and easy maintenance appealing. At the same time, a professional couple may prefer the sophistication and entertainment-friendly features of the Cosmopolitan style. Understanding how each style's unique characteristics can enhance your specific lifestyle needs is key. When practicing your chosen style, prioritize function while maintaining aesthetic cohesion. This might involve adapting traditional style elements to suit modern needs or blending aspects from multiple styles to create the most functional space. For instance, integrating Modern Industrial storage solutions into a Scandinavian-inspired space can provide both robust organization and visual serenity.

EXPLORING THE SEVEN ESSENTIAL MODERN DESIGN STYLES

MODERNISM

Modernism celebrates clean lines and functional beauty. This style emphasizes: open floor plans that promote flow, minimal ornamentation station, integration of natural light emphasis on function natural materials, built-in storage solutions.

Visual Elements: Clean lined furniture, neutral color palette, large window, intergrated storage, natural material finishes

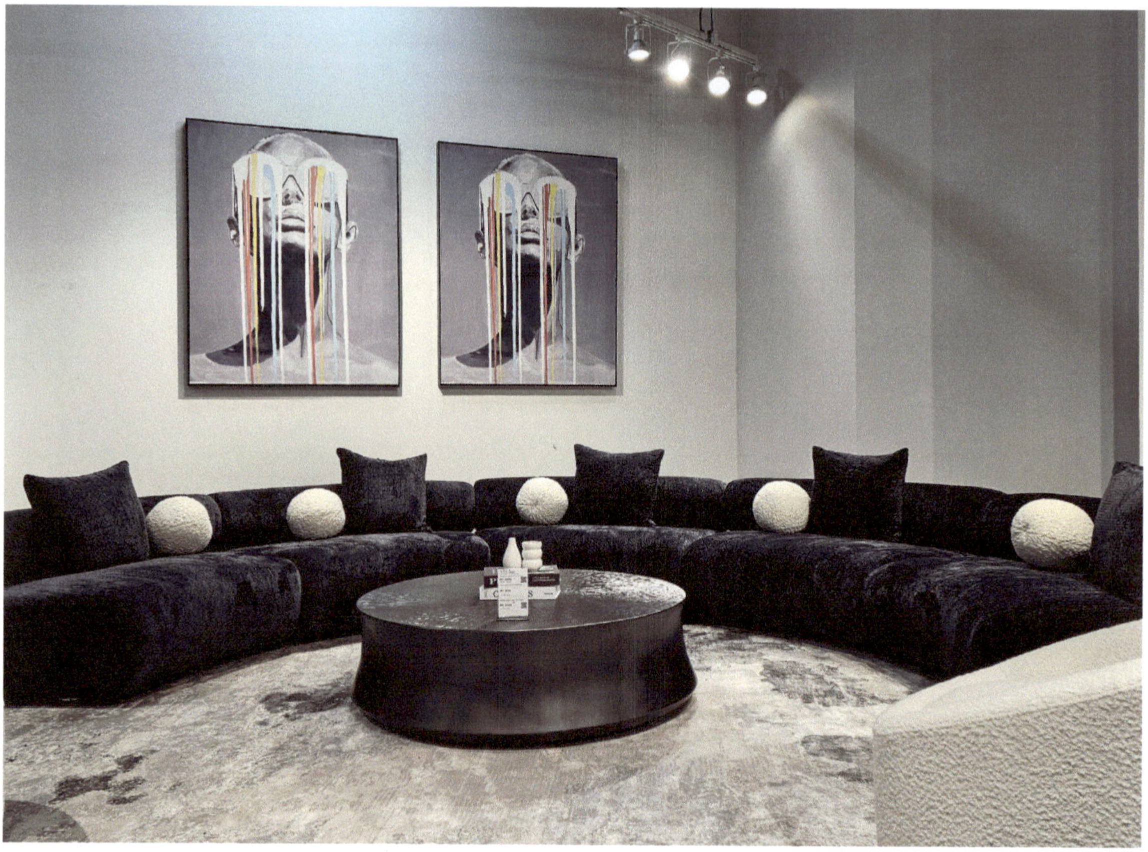

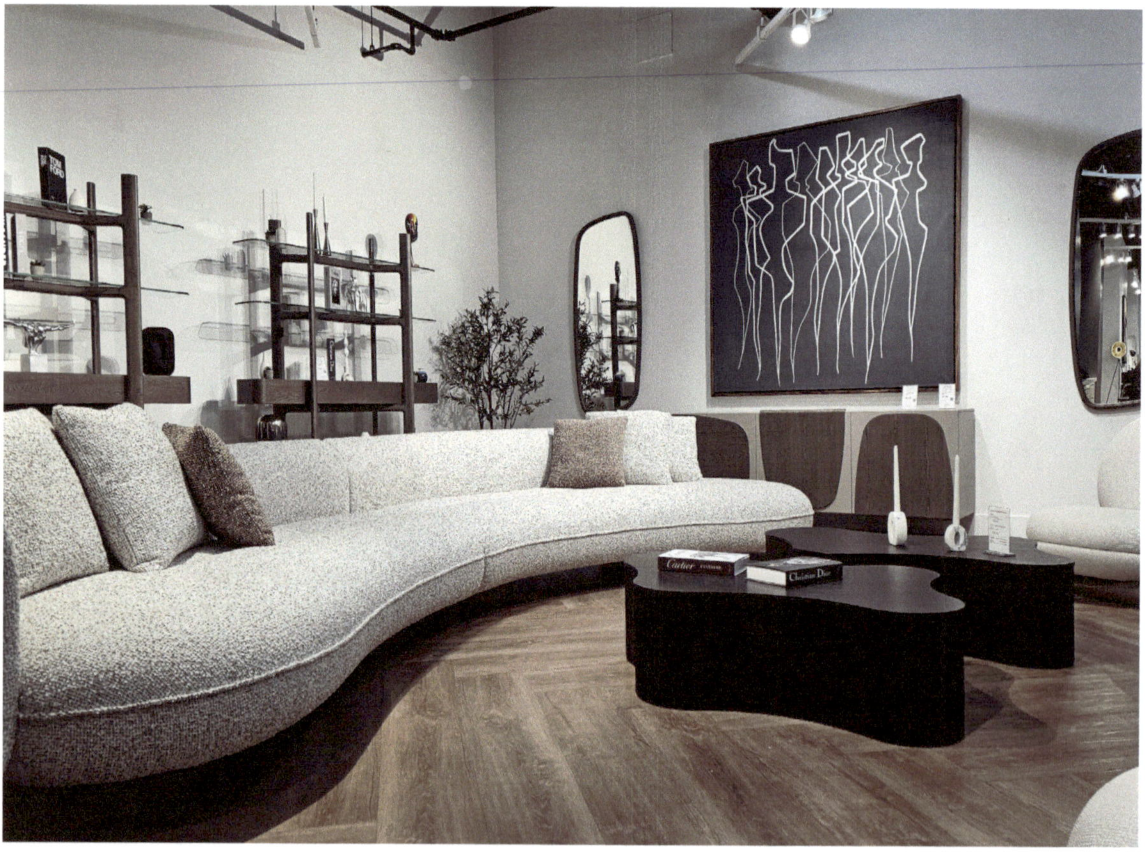
Cartier
Christian Dior

MODERN INDUSTRIAL

This style celebrates architectural elements while creating adaptable spaces: exposed structural features raw material finishes high ceilings mixed material palette factory-style windows

Visual Elements: Exposed brick walls, metal fixtures, concrete floors, industrial lighting and open ductwork.

MODERN RANCH

Bringing Contemporary comfort to traditional ranch design: single-level, living indoor-outdoor connection, vaulted ceilings, natural materials extended eaves.

Visual Elements: open-concept layout, large sliding doors, natural stone features, wood beam ceilings and outdoor living spaces.

SCANDINAVIAN

This design emphasizes lightness, functionality, and natural elements: light wood tones, White walls, Natural textiles, Simple forms, and Organized Storage.

Visual Elements: Light wood floors, White walls, Minimalist furniture, Natural textiles and Functional storage

COSMOPOLITAN STYLE

The Cosmopolitan style embodies sophisticated urban living, combining luxury with practicality while drawing inspiration from international design influences. This style particularly suits those who appreciate refined aesthetics and enjoy entertaining, creating spaces that feel both elegant and welcoming.

Visual Characteristics:

- Dramatic lighting features that create ambiance and focal points.
- Rich material combinations, including marble, glass, and metals.
- Bold architectural details that define spaces.
- High-contrast color schemes that create visual interest.
- Curated art pieces that add personality and sophistication.

Key Features:

- Statement lighting fixtures, often featuring crystal or metallic elements
- Custom built-in cabinetry with sophisticated finishes
- High-end appliances integrated seamlessly into the design
- Mixed metal finishes that add depth and interest
- Textural contrasts between smooth and rough surfaces
- Smart home technology discreetly incorporated
- Luxury materials used strategically as focal points
- Art gallery-style lighting systems
- Floor-to-ceiling windows with dramatic window treatments
- Elegant storage solutions that maintain clean lines

Ideal Applications: Living rooms feature conversation areas with carefully curated furniture pieces, while kitchens combine professionalgrade appliances with elegant finishes. Bathrooms often include spa-like amenities, and bedrooms create sanctuary-like atmospheres with premium materials and lighting.

MINIMALISM

Minimalism takes the "less is more" philosophy to its purest form, creating spaces where every element serves a clear purpose and beauty emerges from simplicity. This style excels in creating calm, uncluttered environments that promote focus and tranquility.

Visual Characteristics:

- Extreme simplicity in all design elements
- Monochromatic or limited color palettes
- Hidden storage solutions that maintain clean lines
- Precise geometric forms and proportions
- Emphasis on negative space and visual breathing room

Key Features:

- Flush cabinet doors without visible hardware
- Integrated appliances that disappear into walls
- Concealed storage systems behind smooth surfaces
- Minimal trim and architectural details
- Strategic use of lighting to enhance form
- Single material used consistently throughout spaces
- Floating elements that create visual lightness
- Precise alignments and symmetry
- Invisible technology integration
- Seamless transitions between spaces

Ideal Applications:

Kitchens feature handleless cabinetry and integrated appliances while living spaces maintain clear sight lines with carefully selected furniture. Bedrooms create serene environments through simplified design elements, and bathrooms offer spa-like simplicity.

MODERN ZEN

Modern Zen style creates peaceful, contemplative spaces by combining traditional Japanese design principles with contemporary comfort. This style particularly benefits those seeking to create calm, balanced environments that support mental well-being while maintaining modern functionality.

Visual Characteristics:

- Natural material focus with emphasis on wood and stone
- Balanced compositions that create visual harmony
- Abundant natural Light with controlled distribution
- Neutral color palettes inspired by nature
- Simple, clean lines with organic influences

Key Features:

- Water features that add sound and movement
- Natural stone elements that ground spaces
- Simple furniture forms without ornamentation
- Indoor plants as integral design elements
- Sliding screens for flexible space division
- Diffused lighting that creates soft atmospheres
- Tatami-inspired flooring areas
- Meditation spaces integrated into the design
- Indoor-outdoor connections
- Natural ventilation systems

Ideal Applications:

Living areas feature low-profile furniture and natural materials, while the bedrooms create sanctuary-like spaces with minimal distractions. Bathrooms incorporate spa inspired elements, and transitional spaces use sliding panels for flexible room definition. Each of these styles offers unique benefits for modern living while maintaining distinct design principles.

Cosmopolitan style suits those who:
- Appreciate refined elegance
- Enjoy entertaining
- Value sophisticated details
- Prefer urban aesthetics
- Embrace luxury materials

Minimalism benefits those who:
- Seek visual calm
- Prefer organized environments
- Value simplicity
- Appreciate precise details
- Want reduced maintenance

Modern style supports those who:
- Prioritize tranquility
- Value natural elements
- Seek balance in design
- Appreciate subtle details
- Want contemplative spaces

When implementing these styles, consider how their characteristics align with your lifestyle needs and maintenance preferences. The most successful applications often come from understanding not just how a style looks but how it supports and enhances daily living patterns.

EXPLORING THE SEVEN ESSENTIAL MODERN DESIGN STYLES

Below is a summary table outlining the key features of each design style:

Style	Key Features	Best For	Materials	Color Palette
Modernism	Clean lines, open spaces	Minimalists	Glass, steel, wood	Neutral with bold accents
Modern Industrial	Raw elements, high ceilings	Urban dwellers	Brick, metal, concrete	Grays, browns, blacks
Modern Ranch	Indoor-outdoor flow	Nature lovers	Stone, wood, glass	Earth tones
Scandinavian	Light, airy spaces	Organization enthusiasts	Light woods, natural fibers	Whites, pale woods
Cosmopolitan	Luxe finishes, global influences	Entertainers	Marble, metals	Rich, dramatic
Minimalism	Essential elements, decluttered	Simplicity seekers	Seamless materials	Monochromatic
Modern Zen	Natural harmony, tranquility	Peace seekers	Bamboo, stone	Natural neutrals

MODERNISM IMPLEMENTATION

The successful implementation of modernist design requires careful attention to both materials and spatial relationships. Begin by thoroughly assessing your space's natural light patterns, which will inform furniture placement and room layouts. Consider how sunlight moves through your space throughout the day and plan accordingly to enhance the space's flow and ambiance.

Material Selection Guidelines:

Natural materials should highlight their inherent qualities. Choose wood with clear grain patterns, stones with natural variations, and metals with consistent finishes. Every material should serve both a functional and aesthetic purpose. For example, select flooring materials that create visual continuity while providing appropriate durability for the space's intended use.

Colour Implementation:

Start with a neutral base palette of whites, greys, and earth tones. These colours should have subtle undertones that complement the materials you've chosen. Add selective colour accents through artwork or key furniture pieces to maintain balance but use restraint. The goal is to create a serene backdrop that highlights architectural features and invites natural light into the space.

Furniture Specifications:

Opt for furniture with clean lines and minimal ornamentation. Pieces should appear to float in space, often achieved by incorporating raised legs or wall-mounted designs. Follow these specific guidelines for furniture height and spacing:

SpacingRequirements:

Walkways: Minimum 36 inches

Seating groups: 8–12 feet diameter

Dining areas: 36 inches from table to wall

Seating Height:

- Dining chairs: 16–18 inches.
- Living room seating: 17–19 inches
- Occasional chairs: 15–17 inches

MODERN INDUSTRIAL DESIGN DESIGN IMPLEMENTATION

Industrial style is characterized by a balance between raw, unfinished elements and refined finishes. Identify architectural features worth highlighting, such as exposed beams, brick walls, or concrete surfaces. These elements will guide your material and colour choices throughout the space.

Surface Treatment Guidelines:

Ensure authenticity in material finishes while considering practicality. For example: Concrete floors should be sealed with penetrating sealers that protect them while maintaining their natural appearance. Exposed brick should be treated with breathable sealers to prevent dust while preserving the texture.

Metal elements should receive appropriate anti-corrosion treatments that enhance, rather than mask, their natural patina.

Material Selection Matrix

Understanding material compatibility ensures successful implementation across different design styles. This comprehensive matrix helps guide material selections based on style requirements and practical considerations.

Lighting Specifications:

Layer lighting to create a harmonious balance between ambience and functionality. Consider the following lighting requirements: Task Lighting: 50-75 footcandles for work areas. Ambient Lighting: 20-30 footcandles for general spaces Accent Lighting: 3x ambient lighting for highlighted features

Modern Minimalist Materials:

Primary Surfaces: Low-maintenance engineered materials.

- Accent Elements: natural stone, clear glass
- Hardware: hidden or integrated
- Finishes: matte or subtle sheen
- Durability Ratings (1-5 scale)
- Daily use areas: minimum 4
- Light use areas: minimum 3
- Accent pieces: minimum 3

Maintenance Requirements:
- Daily: Quick dusting
- Weekly: Thorough cleaning
- Monthly: Protective treatment renewal
- Annually: Professional assessment
- Budget Planning Tools
- Cost Estimation Framework
- Develop accurate budgets by considering both immediate costs and long-term value. This framework helps Effectively across different project aspects. allocate resources
- Base Construction Costs (per square foot):
- Light Renovation: $100-150
- Moderate Renovation: $200-300
- Extensive Renovation: $400-500
- Luxury Renovation: $500+
- Material Cost Allocation:
- Flooring: 15-20% of materials budget
- Cabinetry: 25-30% of materials budget
- Fixtures: 10-15% of materials budget
- Finishes: 15-20% of materials budget
- Lighting: 10-15% of materials budget

CHAPTER

04

PLANNING YOUR PURPOSE-DRIVEN PROJECT

Successful renovation projects require careful planning, ensuring design decisions align with practical implementation.

A professional project plan considers the desired outcome and the entire journey—from concept to completion. It ensures that each phase supports the overall goals, minimizes disruption, and optimizes resources.

Planning begins with establishing clear project objectives that reflect immediate needs and long-term aspirations. These objectives should define your goals and explain why these changes are important to your daily life. For example, rather than simply stating, "Update the kitchen," specify functional improvements like "create an efficient workflow for meal preparation while accommodating family gatherings."

1. Timeline Development

Timeline development requires understanding the sequence of activities and their interdependencies. A professional plan considers construction time and all project phases, including design development, permitting, material selection, and procurement. Allow ample time for decision-making and potential adjustments. Rushing choices often leads to compromises that undermine long-term satisfaction.

2. Budget Planning

Budget planning must consider all project aspects, including obvious and hidden costs. Beyond construction expenses, consider costs for temporary living arrangements during renovation, potential utility upgrades, and professional services. Building a contingency fund (15-20% of your total budget) helps manage unexpected conditions without derailing the project.

3. Material and Finish Selections

Material and finish selections require careful consideration of both immediate impact and long-term performance. Professional planning evaluates materials based on multiple criteria, including durability, maintenance requirements, environmental impact, and cost-effectiveness. Consider how materials will age and perform under your specific living conditions.

4. Professional Selection

The selection of professionals should align with your project's specific requirements. Beyond verifying credentials and references, assess communication styles and problem-solving approaches. The most successful projects often arise from strong, collaborative relationships between homeowners and their professional teams.

5. Documentation

Documentation plays a crucial role in project success. Maintain detailed records of all decisions, including the rationale behind your choices and any alternatives considered. This information is invaluable during implementation and helps inform future maintenance and updates.

6. Impact on Daily Life

Consider how the renovation process will impact your daily life and plan accordingly. Develop strategies for maintaining essential functions during construction, whether through temporary arrangements or carefully planned project phasing. Professional planning anticipates disruptions and creates solutions before problems arise.

7. Technology Integration

Technology integration should be considered early in the planning process, even if implementation happens later. Ensure that your home's infrastructure supports current needs and future possibilities. This might involve running conduits for wiring or planning space for future system additions.

8. Environmental Responsibility

Environmental responsibility should inform all planning decisions. Consider energy efficiency, resource conservation, and waste reduction throughout the project.

Sustainable choices often provide environmental benefits and long-term savings through reduced operational expenses.

Project Planning Phase Summary

To ensure success in your renovation project, follow this structured approach:

- Room selection and Priority
- Evaluate the impact on daily life
- Consider seasonal timing
- Assess complexity level
- Plan for displacement
- Coordinate with other projects
- Budget development
- Research current market costs
- Include contingency funds
- Account for temporary arrangements
- Consider long-term value
- Plan for unexpected discoveries
- Style selection
- Align with lifestyle needs
- Consider maintenance requirements
- Evaluate longevity
- Test material samples
- Plan color schemes
- Research and resources
- Collect inspiration images
- Source material samples
- Verify contractor availability

Before beginning your renovation:

- Finalize design plans
- Secure necessary permits
- Confirm contractor schedules
- Order critical materials
- Arrange temporary living solutions if needed
- Document existing conditions
- Create contingency plans
- Establish communication protocols
- Set up dust containment
- Review safety procedures

This structured approach ensures that all crucial elements are considered and planned for before work begins, helping to prevent delays and minimize surprises during the renovation process.

- Check permit requirements
- Review building codes
- Essential elements
- List non-negotiable features
- Prioritize functionality
- Consider future needs
- Evaluate energy efficiency
- Plan storage requirements
- Preparation Steps
- Clear work areas
- Protect remaining spaces
- Arrange temporary solutions
- Schedule deliveries
- Plan waste management
- Implementation checklist

Project Timeline Development

Create realistic project timelines by understanding the sequence and duration of different implementation phases.

- Pre-construction phase:
- Design development: 4-6 weeks
- Material selection: 2-3 weeks
- Contractor selection: 2-3 weeks
- Permitting: 3-8 weeks
- Construction phase:
- Site preparation: 1 week
- Major construction: 6-12 weeks
- Finish work: 2-4 weeks
- Final details: 1-2 weeks

CHAPTER 05

BUDGETING WITH PURPOSE

Understanding how to allocate resources effectively is key to ensuring that your renovation meets your goals while staying within budget. Professional budgeting begins not with numbers but with a thorough assessment of how you live in your space and which elements will most significantly enhance your daily life.

Identifying Must-Have Elements

The foundation of purpose-driven budgeting is understanding which elements are essential to supporting your lifestyle. Start by considering how you use your space and which features would most impact your daily activities. For example, a family that frequently entertains may prioritize their budget differently than one focused on quiet, personal spaces.

For the enthusiastic home chef and entertainer, essential elements might include:

Professional-grade cooking appliances that offer precise temperature control and multiple cooking zones.

Extensive counter space for food preparation and buffet-style serving. A well-designed bar area for beverage service and casual gatherings.

Flexible furniture arrangements that allow for easy movement and conversation.

Enhanced ventilation systems to manage cooking odor and maintain comfort.

Strategic lighting that adapts to diffifferent entertaining scenarios.

By understanding these priorities, you can allocate your budget resources more effectively. For example, investing in top-tier appliances might mean selecting more moderate options for other elements while maintaining overall quality. This approach ensures that the features most important to your lifestyle receive the appropriate investment.

Strategic Budget Allocation

Once you've identified your must-have elements, develop a budget that prioritizes these features while maintaining balance throughout the project. Consider both immediate functionality and long-term value. High-quality appliances warrant a larger portion of the budget because they directly impact daily activities and typically offer better longevity.

When planning your budget, consider how different elements interact. For example, a professional-grade range may require upgraded electrical systems or enhanced ventilation. Including these related costs in your initial budget helps avoid surprises during renovation. Similarly, investing in quality cabinetry and storage solutions can maximize the functionality of your appliances and entertaining spaces.

Value Engineering for Priority Items

Professional budgeting often involves strategic decisions about where to make significant investments and where more moderate solutions might suffice. For example, if entertaining is a priority in your renovation, consider:

Investing heavily in kitchen workflow and appliances:
Choosing durable, easy-to-clean surfaces for high-traffic areas Selecting flexible lighting systems that can enhance various activities. Prioritizing quality ventilation and climate control focusing on open-concept design elements that facilitate gathering estimated cost breakdown with priority considerations.

KITCHEN RENOVATION WITH ENTERTAINMENT FOCUS

- Professional appliances: $15,000 - $40,000
- Pro-grade range: $8,000 - $15,000
- Refrigeration: $5,000 - $12,000
- Wine storage: $2,000 - $8,000
- Dishwasher(s): $1,200 - $5,000
- Cabinetry and storage: $20,000 - $45,000
- Main cabinetry: $15,000 - $30,000
- Special storage solutions: $3,000 - $8,000
- Bar area cabinetry: $2,000 - $7,000
- Countertops and surfaces: $8,000 - $15,000
- Main countertops: $5,000 - $10,000
- Bar surfaces: $2,000 - $3,000
- Backsplash: $2,000 - $5,000
- Lighting systems: $3,000 - $8,000
- Task lighting: $1,000 - $2,500
- Ambient lighting: $1,000 - $2,500
- Accent lighting: $1,000 - $3,000
- Ventilation and climate control: $2,500 - $7,000
- Range hood: $1,500 - $4,000
- Additional ventilation: $1,000 - $3,000
- Plumbing and fixtures: $3,000 - $8,000
- Main sink and faucet: $1,000 - $3,000
- Bar sink and faucet: $800 - $2,000
- Water filtration: $1,200 - $3,000 F
- Flooring: $4,000 - $12,000
- Materials: $2,500 - $8,000
- Labor and installation: $20,000 - $45,000
- General contracting: $15,000 - $30,000
- Specialized installation: $5,000 - $15,000
- Total range: $78,500 - $180,000

Contingency Fund

Remember to include a contingency fund of 15-20% above these estimates to accommodate unexpected conditions or desired upgrades that may arise during construction. This ensures that your must-have features can be properly implemented, even if challenges appear during renovation.

Priority-Based Budget Planning

Understanding how different lifestyle priorities influence budget allocation helps create spaces that serve their intended purpose while maintaining fiscal responsibility. Professional budget planning considers immediate functionality and long-term value, adapting standard allocations to specific needs and preferences.

Lifestyle-Based Budget Scenarios

A family that prioritizes cooking and entertaining requires a different budget allocation than one focused on creating a peaceful retreat. Consider how these different priorities influence investment decisions across various aspects of renovation.

THE CHEF'S KITCHEN PRIORITY

When cooking drives renovation decisions, consider investing more substantially in cooking equipments and workspace. A professional-grade range might command $8,000-$15,000 of the budget, but its value extends beyond mere cooking capability. These appliances typically offer superior durability, more precise temperature control, and better energy efficiency than standard options.

Supporting investments include enhanced ventilation systems ($3,000-$6,000), which become crucial with high-perform-ance cooking equipment. Quality ventilation manages cooking odors, helps maintain comfortable temperatures and protects finishes throughout the space. Storage solutions are of particular importance in a chef's kitchen. Consider specialized storage features such as:

Spice organization systems ($800-$1,500)
Knife storage solutions ($400-$800)
Pan organization systems ($600-$1,200)
Pull-out shelving for easy access ($2,000-$4,000)

THE ENTERTAINER'S SPACE

Creating effective, entertaining spaces requires careful consideration of flow and functionality. Invest in flexible furnishings that accommodate different types of gatherings. Consider allocating funds for:

Multi-functional furniture:
- Moveable island units ($1,500-$3,500),
- Comfortable seating with easy-clean fabrics ($3,000-$8,000)
- Storage pieces that double as serving stations ($2,000-$4,000)

Sound and Lighting Systems:
- Integrated audio systems ($3,000-$7,000)
- Programmable lighting scenes ($2,500-$5,000)
- Acoustic treatments ($1,500-$3,500)

COST SAVING ANALYSIS

When certain elements fall outside your primary priorities, consider these professional strategies for maintaining quality while reducing costs:

Alternative Material Selection

Understanding material alternatives helps maintain visual impact while reducing costs in non-priority areas. For example, in less visible areas, consider:

Countertop Options:

Premium: Natural quartzite ($85-$125/sq ft) Mid-range: Quartz composite ($65-$85/sq ft) Budget: Luxury laminate ($35-$45/sq ft)

These alternatives can provide similar aesthetics and functionality at different prices, allowing you to allocate more resources to priority features.

ENERGY EFFICIENCY ANALYSIS

Understanding the long-term cost implications of energy-efficient options helps inform budget decisions:

Lighting Investment Analysis: Initial Cost vs. 10-Year Savings

Standard LED: $15/bulb, saves $150 over a lifetime

Smart LED: $45/bulb, saves $200 over a lifetime

Premium Smart LED: $60/bulb, saves $250 over a lifetime.

Phasing Strategies

Strategic project phasing can help manage budget constraints while ensuring priority elements receive appropriate investment:

Phase 1: Essential infrastructure
- Electrical upgrades
- Plumbing modifications
- Ventilation systems
- Core appliance installation

Phase 2: Functional elements
- Cabinetry
- Countertops
- Flooring
- Basic lighting

Phase 3: Enhancement Features
- Specialty storage
- Advanced lighting
- Smart home integration
- Decorative elements
- Long-Term Value Considerations

Understanding how different investments contribute to long-term value helps inform budget allocation:

APPLIANCE LONGEVITY ANALYSIS

Professional-grade vs. Consumer Models:

- Professional range: 15-20 years, average annual cost $400-600
- Consumer range: 8-12 years, average annual cost $300-400
- Professional refrigerator: 15-20 years, average annual cost $500-700
- Consumer refrigerator: 10-15 years, average annual cost $400-500

Material Durability Impact

Different materials offer varying longevity, affecting long-term value:

Flooring lifespan comparison:
- Hardwood: 50+ years with refinishing every 10-15 years
- Luxury vinyl: 15-25 years with no refinishing required
- Porcelain tile: 50+ years with minimal maintenance
- Natural stone: Lifetime with proper maintenance.

RETURN ON INVESTMENT ANALYSIS

Different improvements offer varying returns on investment:

Kitchen Improvements:
- Major renovation: 60-80% ROI
- Minor renovation: 70-85% ROI
- Appliance upgrade: 60-75% ROI
- Storage solutions: 65-80% ROI

Understanding these returns helps prioritize investments when budget constraints require choices between different improvements.

Home Equity Loans

Traditional financing through home equity loans often provides the most favorable interest rates, typically ranging from 3% to 7%, depending on market conditions and your credit standing. These loans offer the added benefit of tax-deductible interest and longer repayment terms, making managing monthly expenses easier. However, they require sufficient equity in your home and often involve a lengthier approval process.

Construction Loans

Construction loans are a viable option, especially for extensive renovations. These specialized loans typically provide disbursement.

Schedules that align with different construction phases, ensuring proper cash flow throughout the project. While interest rates generally run 1% to 2% higher than traditional mortgages, structured disbursement can help maintain better control over the project's budget and timeline.

Personal Lines of Credit

Personal lines of credit offer flexibility for smaller projects or when quick access to funds is necessary. While interest rates usually range from 8% to 15%, these lines of credit typically have a quicker approval process. They can provide excellent backup funding for unexpected project developments, ensuring you're prepared for unforeseen costs.

Professional Negotiation Strategies

Effective negotiation with contractors and suppliers requires a solid understanding of market conditions and project specifications. Professional negotiation aims to create mutually beneficial agreements that maintain quality while managing costs.

Negotiating with Contractors

When negotiating with contractors, begin by presenting a detailed scope of work that clearly defines expectations. This approach typically reduces bid variations by 15% to 25% and establishes a solid negotiation foundation. Ensure the scope includes specific material requirements, timeline expectations, and quality standards to guarantee accurate pricing.

Negotiating Material Procurement

Material procurement is another area rich with negotiation opportunities. Suppliers often offer 10% to 20% discounts for bulk purchases or when orders are combined across different project phases. Additionally, understanding seasonal pricing fluctuations can help secure additional savings of 5% to 15% on certain materials.

Payment Scheduling and Leverage

Payment scheduling is a crucial aspect of negotiations. Structuring payments to align with project milestones ensures fair terms for all parties and provides leverage to ensure quality completion. Consider retaining 10% to 15% of payment until the satisfactory completion of punch list items. This can be a powerful motivator for contractors to finish the project according to the agreed-upon standards.

QUALITY ASSESSMENT FRAMEWORK

Maintaining high standards throughout implementation requires systematic quality assessment protocols. Professional quality management considers both immediate appearance and long-term performance.

Material assessment begins before installation. Establish clear acceptance criteria for delivered materials, including:

- Natural stone evaluation standards
- Color variation within the specified range
- Structural integrity without fissures
- Consistent thickness within 1/16 inch
- Proper sealing and finish application
- Complete documentation of origin and grade
- Installation quality requires ongoing monitoring

Professional inspection protocols typically include the following:

- Daily installation reviews
- Surface preparation completeness
- Material alignment and spacing
- Proper adhesive application
- Joint consistency
- Surface protection measures

Risk Management Implementation

- Effective risk management protects both project success and investment value.
- Professional risk management strategies address potential challenges before they impact project outcomes.

Weather-related risks require specific mitigation strategies. For exterior work, maintain a 15% to 20% buffer in the timeline to accommodate weather delays. Include specific contract language addressing weather-related work stoppages and material protection requirements.

Supply chain disruptions present increasing challenges.

Professional risk management includes:
- Material Risk Mitigation
- Early procurement of long-lead items
- Storage arrangements for early deliveries
- Alternative material specifications
- Multiple supplier relationships
- Clear force majeure contract terms
- Case Studies in Successful Implementation

Understanding how these strategies work in practice provides valuable insights for project planning.

URBAN KITCHEN RENOVATION

Urban Kitchen Renovation: This project faced significant supply chain challenges during implementation. Early identification of potential delays led to proactive material procurement, saving eight weeks in the project timeline and approximately $12,000 in rush fees and temporary arrangements.

Key Success Factors:
- Early material ordering
- Flexible storage arrangements
- Clear communication protocols
- Detailed tracking systems
- Regular supplier updates.

Suburban Whole-House Renovation: This comprehensive project demonstrated effective risk management through careful phase planning and strategic material procurement. Implementation Highlights:
- Phase-based material ordering
- Weather-conscious scheduling
- Multiple supplier relationships
- Detailed quality protocols
- Regular milestone assessments
- Timeline management integration

Professional timeline management integrates with all aspects of the implementation strategy.

Critical Path Analysis: Successful projects typically focus on critical path elements while allowing flexibility in non-critical activities. This approach often reduces project duration by 15% to 20% while maintaining quality standards.

Timeline Integration Strategy:
- Clear milestone definitions
- Regular progress assessments
- Proactive delay mitigation
- Resource coordination
- Communication protocols

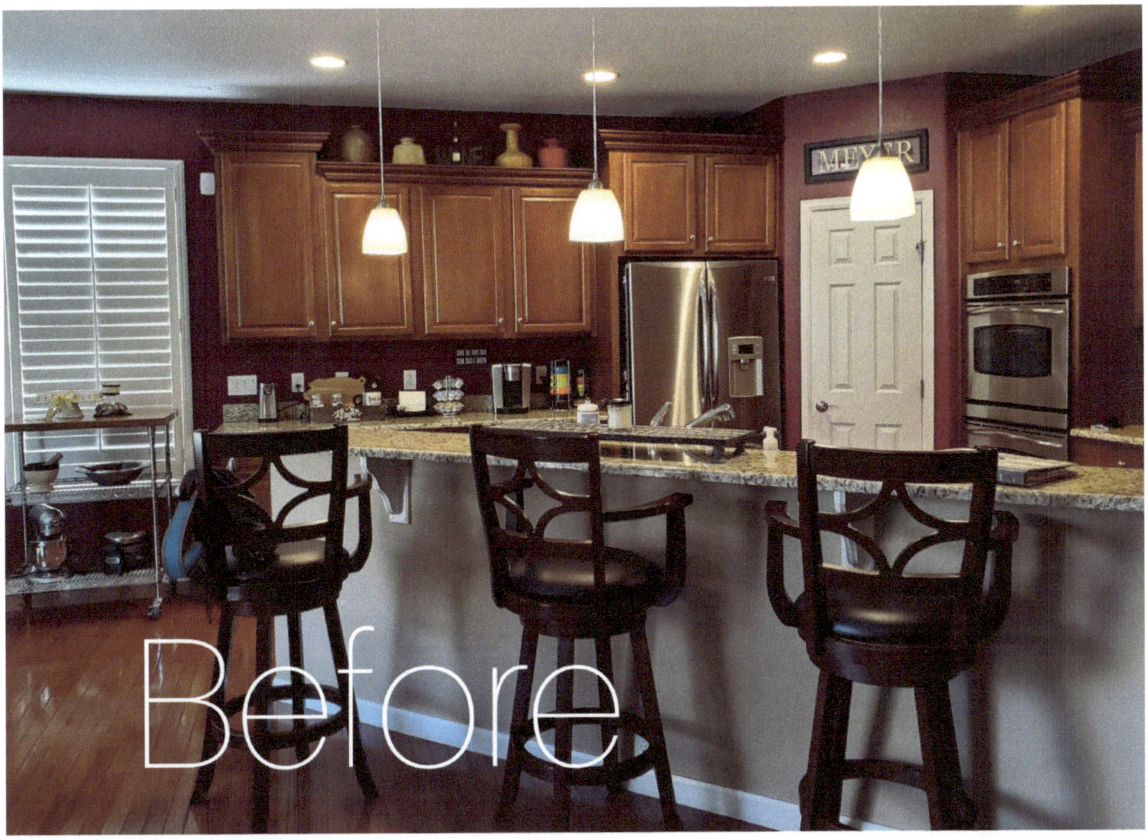
Before

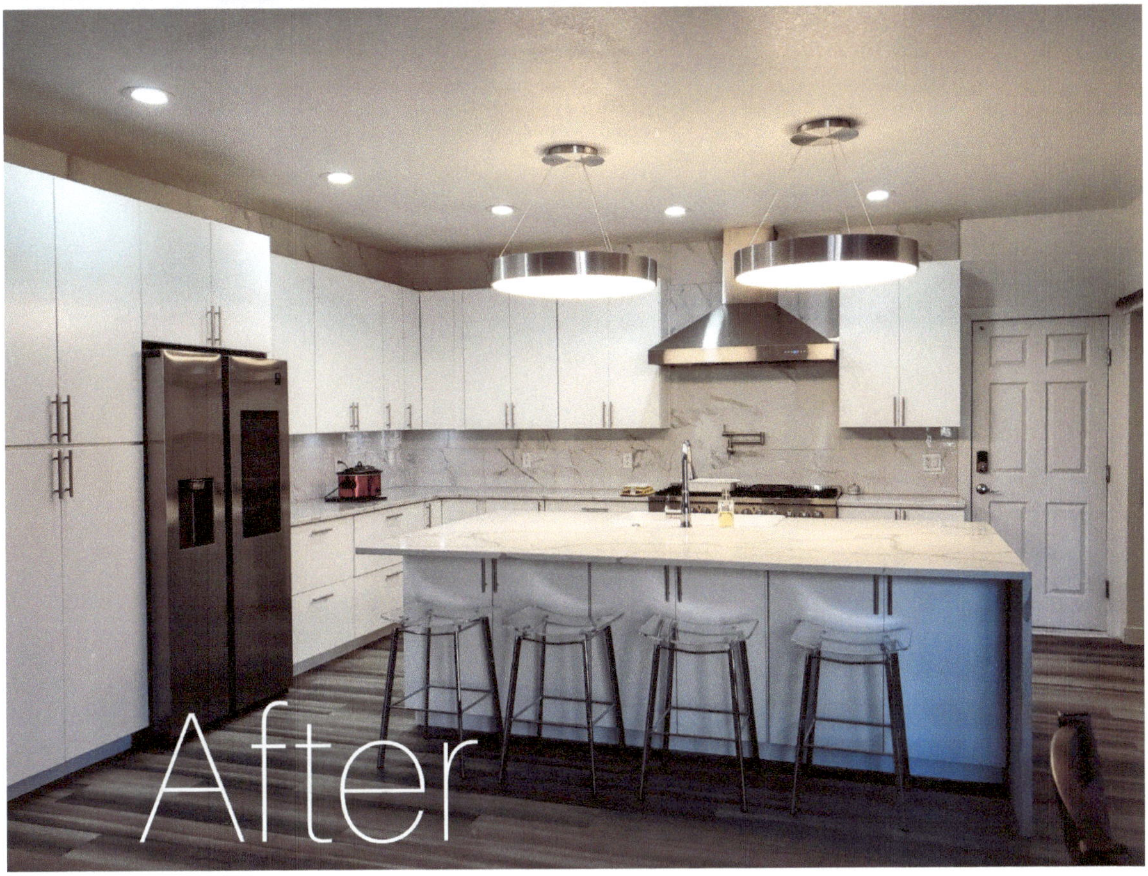
After

CHAPTER

06

WORKING WITH PROFESSIONALS

Selecting and collaborating with design and construction professionals requires both understanding their technical qualifications and evaluating their communication styles. The partnerships you form with these professionals are essential for the success of your renovation project, making careful selection and effective collaboration critical.

Understanding Different Professional Roles

Each professional in the design and construction process brings a unique set of skills and perspectives. Architects, Interior Designers, and Contractors all play distinct roles in a renovation. Some projects may require input from all three, while others may only need one or two. The key is understanding which professionals will best serve your specific needs and ensuring the right expertise is applied to each aspect of the project.

Evaluating Professional Credentials and Soft Skills

Professional credentials, such as licenses and certifications, are important indicators of expertise and commitment to industry standards. However, credentials alone don't guarantee a successful partnership. It's equally important to assess how well potential partners understand your goals, communicate their ideas, and demonstrate problem-solving abilities. These "soft skills" often prove as crucial as technical expertise to ensure a smooth collaboration.

The Importance of Effective Communication

Clear and consistent communication is the foundation of any successful professional relationship. Make sure that decisions are documented, that regular progress updates are provided and that established channels are in place for addressing questions and concerns. Open, honest dialogue throughout the project helps prevent misunderstandings and keeps the project on track.

Contract Development and Understanding Responsibilities Contract development is another critical aspect of working with professionals. Pay close attention to the contract's scope, timeline expectations, and payment terms. A well-written agreement will delineate responsibilities, establish communication protocols, and define project milestones. Understanding these details thoroughly before signing the contract can help prevent misunderstandings and disputes.

Professional Associations and Resources

- American Society of Interior Designers (ASID) Certification standards.
- Professional Development Design Resources
- Project guidance

Member directory Website: www.asid.org

American Institute of Architects (AIA)

- Professional standards
- Technical resources
- Contract documents
- Project tools

Find an architect. Website: www.aia.org

National Kitchen and Bath Association (NKBA)

- Design guidelines
- Technical standards
- Professional certification
- Industry research

Member directory Website: www.nkba.org

NationalAssociation of Home Builders (NAHB)

- Construction standards
- Technical resources
- Professional development
- Industry research

Contractor directory Website: www.nahb.org

Additional Professional Resources:

- Building Green (Sustainable design resources) Construction Specifications Institute
  https://www.csireasources.org/learning/practiceguides/sdcpg
  (Technical standards)
- International Interior Design Association
  https://iida.org
  (Professional network)
- U.S. Green Building Council (Sustainability guidelines). https://www.usgbc.org
- Residential Energy Services Network (Energy efficiency standards) https://www.theseedcenter.org

Professional Selection Guide

Selecting design and construction professionals requires systematic evaluation of technical capabilities and interpersonal skills.

This comprehensive guide outlines the key criteria and processes for making informed selection and evaluation criteria for Design Professionals.

When evaluating potential design professionals, consider their expertise in several key areas. While technical proficiency is essential, a successful partnership depends on qualities that foster effective collaboration.

Assessing Technical Qualifications

A professional designer should thoroughly understand current design principles, building codes, and construction methods. Review their portfolio to find projects similar in scope and style to yours. Please pay close attention to how they have addressed design challenges similar to those you anticipate in your project.

Evaluating Communication Skills

Clear and effective communication is crucial throughout the design and construction process. During initial consultations, observe how well the professional listens to your needs and explains their ideas. They should be able to translate technical concepts into simple, understandable terms and be open to answering your questions thoroughly.

Interview Protocol

Initial Consultation Questions:
- "Could you walk me through your typical design process?"
- "How do you handle changes or unexpected issues during a project?"
- "What is your experience with projects similar to mine?" "How do you typically structure communication during projects?"
- "Could you explain your fee structure and billing practices?"
- Follow-up Evaluation Points: Timeliness of response to initial inquiry
- Thoroughness of questions about your project quality of reference materials provided professionalism of presentation materials
- Clarity of the proposed timeline and process Contract Development Guide.

Professional contracts provide essential protection for all parties while establishing clear expectations for project execution. This guide outlines key elements that should be included in professional service agreements.

ESSENTIAL CONTRACT ELEMENTS

Scope Definition:

The contract should delineate all services, including specific deliverables and excluded items. This section must define professional responsibility boundaries and identify owner-provided items or services.

Timeline Specifications:

Include both overall project duration and specific milestone dates. The contract should address:
- Design development phase duration
- Review and revision periods
- Construction document preparation
- Permit application timing
- Construction phase services
- Project completion criteria

Payment Terms:

Establish clear payment schedules tied to project milestones. Include:
- Initial deposit requirements
- Progress payment timing
- Completion payment conditions
- Change order pricing methods
- Reimbursable expense policies
- Quality control standards

Maintaining high standards throughout project execution requires systematic quality control processes. These guidelines establish frameworks for ensuring consistent quality at every project phase.

Design Quality Control:

Document Review Process: Each phase of design development should undergo systematic review:
- Concept development
- Alignment with project goals
- Feasibility assessment
- Budget compliance review
- Code compliance check
- Timeline verification
- Design development
- Material specification review
- System integration check
- Construction detail verification
- Coordination between disciplines
- Cost estimate reconciliation
- Construction quality control

Implementation Monitoring:

Regular site inspections should verify the following:
- Material quality
- Conformance to specifications
- Proper storage and handling
- Installation methods
- Finish quality
- System integration
- Workmanship standards
- Installation precision detail execution
- Surface Preparation
- Finish application clean-up quality

Communication protocols

Effective project communication requires established protocols that ensure all parties remain informed while maintaining efficient information flow.
- Regular Communication Schedule
- Weekly updates:
- Progress summary
- Decision items pending
- Schedule updates
- Budget status
- Quality concerns
- Monthly reviews:
- Detailed progress assessment
- Budget reconciliation
- Timeline evaluation
- Risk assessment
- Resource planning
- Documentation requirements

Project Documentation:

Maintain systematic records of Design Decisions:
- Option evaluations
- Selection rationale
- Cost implications

- Timeline impacts
- Implementation requirements
- Construction Progress:
- Daily work logs
- Material deliveries
- Quality inspections
- Issue resolution
- Change orders

Change Management Procedures

Changes during project execution require careful management to maintain budget control and timeline integrity. These procedures establish frameworks for handling modifications effectively. Change Order Process.

Evaluation Protocol:

- Each proposed change requires an assessment of Cost implications
- Schedule Impacts design integration
- System affects
- Quality Implications.

Documentation Requirements:

Change orders must include a detailed scope description

- Cost breakdown
- Timeline adjustment
- Material specifications
- Approval signatures

CHAPTER

07

MANAGING YOUR RENOVATION PROJECT

Successfully executing a renovation project requires a systematic management approach that anticipates challenges while focusing on the desired outcomes. Professional project management combines careful planning with flexibility, ensuring your renovation progresses efficiently while upholding quality standards. Establishing clear project governance is the foundation of successful management. This begins with defining decision-making protocols and communication channels to guide the renovation process. As the project owner, you must balance oversight with allowing professionals the autonomy to execute their responsibilities effectively.

Daily project oversight requires attention to several key areas. Progress monitoring should include regular documentation of completed work, material deliveries, and any issues that require attention. Professional project management maintains detailed records, providing a clear picture of the project's status and crucial documentation for future reference.

Quality control is a fundamental aspect of project management. It extends beyond inspecting finished work, verifying proper material storage installation methods, and protecting completed areas. Regular quality assessments help identify potential issues before they impact the project's outcome.

Timeline management requires understanding the interdependencies of different project phases.

For example, cabinet installation cannot proceed until the walls are finished, and appliance delivery must be coordinated with cabinet completion. Professional management Ensures awareness of these relationships while adjusting schedules to accommodate changes without disrupting the workflow.

Budget oversight demands continuous attention throughout the project. This includes tracking direct and indirect expenses that affect overall project economics. Professional management involves maintaining detailed cost records and regularly comparing actual expenses against budgeted amounts to identify potential variances early.

Change management presents unique challenges in renovation projects. Even the most carefully planned projects may require adjustments. Professional management involves established protocols for evaluating proposed changes, assessing their impact on the budget and timeline, and implementing approved modifications while maintaining project momentum.

Contractor coordination requires careful scheduling and access management. Different trades may need to work in the same areas simultaneously, requiring precise orchestration to maintain efficiency. Professional management ensures proper work sequencing while maintaining clear communication between all parties.

Material management extends beyond initial selection to include verification of deliveries, proper storage, and timely availability for installation. Professional management maintains detailed material.

Specifications and quantities records while coordinating delivery schedules with installation timelines.

Thorough documentation throughout the project creates valuable resources for future reference. This includes maintaining records of approved changes, installation details, and warranty information. Professional management ensures comprehensive documentation of all significant project elements, providing a reliable reference for future maintenance or modifications.

CHAPTER

08

SMART HOME INTEGRATION

Modern home design increasingly incorporates technology that enhances functionality while improving efficiency. Understanding how to properly integrate smart systems ensures that technology truly serves your needs while maintaining long-term adaptability. Infrastructure planning forms the foundation of successful smart home integration. This begins with ensuring adequate electrical and network capacity to support current and future needs. Professional integration involves carefully evaluating power requirements, and data transmission needs while planning appropriate distribution systems.

Network design requires particular attention in modern homes. Beyond basic internet connectivity, smart home systems often rely on robust local networks that support multiple devices while maintaining security. Professional integration involves careful consideration of wireless coverage, backup systems, and security protocols.

Control system selection significantly impacts daily interaction with smart home features. Whether using voice commands, touchscreens, or mobile devices, the interface should provide intuitive operation while maintaining reliability. Professional integration considers both immediate usability and long-term support requirements. Lighting control is often a cornerstone of smart home functionality. Modern systems can adjust automatically based on time of day, occupancy, or specific activities. Professional integration ensures proper fixture selection and wiring while establishing programming that enhances daily living patterns.

Climate management through smart system offers both comfort and efficiency benefits. Advanced temperature control can adjust automatically based on occupancy patterns while optimizing energy usage. Professional integration includes careful sensor placement and system programming to balance comfort with efficiency. Security integration requires careful attention to both technological capabilities and practical implementation. Modern systems can include video monitoring, access control, and environmental sensors. Professional integration ensures proper component selection and placement while maintaining appropriate security protocols.

Entertainment systems are increasingly connected with other home technologies. Modern setups may adjust lighting and temperature for optimal viewing while managing sound distribution throughout the home. Professional integration ensures proper component selection and placement while maintaining flexible control options.

Energy management has become more sophisticated with smart home integration. Modern systems can monitor consumption patterns and automatically adjust operations to optimize efficiency. Professional integration includes carefully selecting compatible components while establishing monitoring and control protocols. Future adaptability requires careful consideration during the initial system design. As technology evolves rapidly, flexibility in basic infrastructure is crucial. Professional integration involves planning for future expansion while maintaining documentation that facilitates system updates.

SUMMARY RECOMMENDATIONS FOR SMART INTEGRATION

Professionals should consider the following core elements for successful smart home integration:

- Infrastructure planning to support both current and future technology.
- Strong network design with adequate security measures.
- User-friendly control systems for seamless operation.
- Smart lighting solutions that enhance efficiency and comfort.
- Climate control systems optimized for energy savings and convenience.
- Comprehensive security measures, including video monitoring and access control.
- Integrated entertainment systems that connect with other smart home features.
- Energy management solutions to monitor and optimize consumption.
- Future-proofing strategies to allow easy system upgrades and expansions.

By addressing these elements, homeowners and professionals can ensure that smart home technology enhances everyday living while maintaining efficiency, security, and long-term adaptability.

Essential Infrastructure:

- Robust electrical systems with adequate capacity Comprehensive network coverage throughout the home
- Secure data transmission protocols
- Reliable backup power systems
- Clear documentation of all installations

Core Functionality

- Intuitive control interfaces
- Automated lighting management
- Efficient climate control
- Integrated security systems
- Energy consumption monitoring
- Detailed Material Guide and Cost Analysis

Material Categories and Specifications
1. Flooring Materials

- Premium options:
- Hardwood: $12-20/sq ft
- White oak
- Walnut
- Reclaimed wood
- Bamboo (sustainable)
- Cork (sustainable)

Mid-Range Options:
- Luxury vinyl plank: $5-12/sq ft
- Water-resistant
- Durable
- Easy maintenance

Sustainable Options:
- Recycled content Tile: $8-15/sq ft
- Reclaimed wood: $10-25/sq ft
- Bamboo: $5-12/sq ft

2. Wall Coverings

Natural Materials:
- Grass cloth: $30-80/linear yard
- Cork: $25-45/sq ft
- Reclaimed Wood Panels: $15-30/sq ft

Modern Options:
- Textured wallpaper: $40-100/roll
- Acoustic panels: $50-150/panel
- Metal panels: $30-80/sq ft

Sustainable Choices:
- Recycled content paper: $35-75/roll
- Natural fiber coverings: $40-90/linear yard
- Zero-VOC finishes: $30-60/gallon

3. Paint Selection

Premium Brands:
- Farrow & ball: $110-140/gallon
- Benjamin moore aura: $70-90/gallon
- Fine Paints of europe: $150-200/gallon

Sustainable Options:
- Zero-VOC formulas: $45-75/gallon
- Natural pigments: $60-100/gallon
- Clay-based paints: $50-80/gallon

4. Countertop Materials

Preferred Sustainable Options:

1. Quartz Cost: $65-125/sq ft installed

Brands:
- Caesarstone
- Silestone
- Cambria

Benefits:
- Non-porous
- Highly durable
- Low maintenance
- Wide color range

2. Butcher Block

Cost: $40-100/sq ft installed

Types:
- End grain
- Edge grain
- Face grain

Benefits:
- Natural antimicrobial
- Repairable
- Warm aesthetic
- Renewable resource

3. PaperStone Composite

Cost: $70-120/sq ft installed

Features:
- Recycled paper content
- Heat resistant
- Non-porous
- Sustainable production

Benefits:
- Environmentally friendly
- Durable
- Unique appearance
- Water-resistant

Recycled Glass:

Cost: $75-125/sq ft installed

Options:
- Vetrazzo
- IceStone
- Curava

Benefits:
- Unique appearance
- Highly durable
- Eco-friendly
- UV resistant

Reclaimed Wood:
Cost: $50-100/sq ft installed

Sources:
- Barn wood
- Industrial beams
- Ship wood

Benefits:
- Character
- Sustainable
- Unique patterns
- Historical value

5. Home Appliances
Premium Brands:
- Wolf/Sub-Zero: $15,000-40,000 (kitchen suite)
- Miele: $12,000-35,000 (kitchen suite)
- Viking: $15,000-35,000 (kitchen suite)

Mid-Range Options:
- Bosch: $8,000-20,000 (kitchen suite)
- ZLINE: $7,000-18,000 (kitchen suite)
- Forno: $6,000-15,000 (kitchen suite)
- Electrolux: $7000-$15000 (kitchen suite)
- Thor: $7000-$15000 (kitchen suite)
- Bertazzoni: $10,000-$20,000 $7000-$15000 (kitchen suite)

Energy-Efficient Focus:
- Energy star rated
- Smart home integration
- Water conservation features

6. Lighting Solutions
Architectural Lighting:
- Recessed: $30-150/fixture
- Track systems: $100-500/system
- Wall washers: $75-300/fixture

Decorative Options:
- Pendants: $150-1,000+/fixture
- Chandeliers: $500-5,000+
- Sconces: $100-800/fixture

Smart Lighting:
- Control Systems: $500-5,000
- LED Integration: $20-100/bulb
- Automated Shading: $300-1,000/window

7. Furniture Selection:
Custom/Designer:
- Sofas: $3,000-10,000
- Dining Tables: $2,000-8,000
- Bedroom Sets: $5,000-15,000

Mid-Range Quality:
- Sofas: $1,500-3,000
- Dining Tables: $1,000-2,000
- Bedroom Sets: $2,500-5,000

Sustainable Options:
- Reclaimed Materials
- FSC-Certified Wood
- Recycled Content Fabrics

Sustainable Materials

RESOURCE DIRECTORY

1. Countertops:
- PaperStone: www.paperstoneproducts.com
- IceStone: www.icestone.com
- Vetrazzo: www.vetrazzo.com

2. Wood Products:
- FSC Directory: www.fsc.org
- Reclaimed Wood: www.reclaimedlumber.org
- Sustainable Woods: www.sustainablewoods.org

3. Eco-Friendly Finishes:
- Green Seal: www.greenseal.org
- Zero-VOC Database: www.greenguard.org
- Natural Finishes: www.earthpigments.com

Professional Organizations

1. Sustainable Design:
- USGBC: www.usgbc.org
- Living Future Institute: www.living-future.org
- Cradle to Cradle: www.c2ccertified.org

2. Material Standards:
- ASTM International: www.astm.org
- Green Building Standards: www.ashrae.org
- Material Testing: www.ul.com

3. Design Resources:
- Interior Design Society: www.interiordesignsociety.org
- Sustainable Furnishings Council: www.sustainablefurnishings.org
- Green Building Alliance: www.go-gba.org

GORDON'S KITCHEN

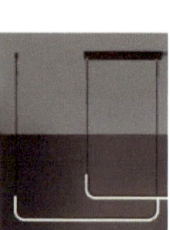

CHAPTER 09

MATERIAL SELECTION AND IMPLEMENTATION

Understanding materials and their applications forms a crucial foundation for successful home design. Professional material selection considers aesthetic appeal, durability, maintenance requirements, and long-term application performance.

Natural Stone Selection

Natural stone offers timeless beauty but requires careful selection based on application. For instance, granite's durability makes it excellent for high-traffic areas, while marble's delicate nature might better suit low-use spaces.

Stone Selection Criteria:

- Density and porosity
- Stain resistance
- Heat tolerance
- Impact resistance
- Maintenance requirements

Kitchen Applications:

Countertops demand particular attention to performance characteristics:

Food preparation areas: Consider acid resistance

Sink areas: Focus on moisture resistance

Cooking zones: Evaluate heat tolerance

Island tops: Assess impact resistance

Backsplashes: Consider ease of cleaning

Engineered Materials

Modern engineered materials often provide superior performance while maintaining aesthetic appeal. Quartz surfaces, for example, offer exceptional durability and minimal maintenance requirements compared to natural stone.

Performance Characteristics:

- Scratch Resistance
- Stain Protection
- UV Stability
- Impact Tolerance
- Chemical Resistance

Application Guidelines:

Different areas require specific material properties:

- High Traffic: Focus on wear resistance
- Wet Areas: Prioritize moisture resistance
- Food Zones: Consider bacterial resistance
- Display Areas: Evaluate UV stability
- Work Surfaces: Assess impact resistance

Wood and Wood Products

Wood brings warmth and natural beauty but requires appropriate species selection and proper finishing for different applications.

Species Selection:

- Hardwoods for durability
- Softwoods for cost efficiency
- Exotic species for unique appearance
- Reclaimed wood for sustainability
- Engineered products for stability

Finishing Requirements:

- Different applications need specific protection:
- High moisture: marine-grade finishes
- UV exposure: sun-resistant coatings
- Heavy use: commercial-grade protection
- Display areas: clear preservation
- Exterior applications: Weather protection

CHAPTER
10

LIGHTING DESIGN FOR PURPOSE

Professional lighting design creates environments that enhance functionality and aesthetics while supporting natural circadian rhythms. Understanding how different lighting types interact helps create spaces that transition smoothly from day to night while maintaining optimal functionality.

Natural Light Integration

Working with natural light requires understanding seasonal variations and daily patterns. The professional design considers how sunlight moves through spaces while planning complementary artificial lighting.

Window Placement Strategy:
- North-facing: diffused, consistent light
- South-facing: strong, direct sunlight
- East-facing: morning brightness
- West-facing: evening intensity
- Skylights: overhead illumination

Light Control Methods:
Different situations require varying approaches:
- Direct sun: UV-filtering films
- Glare: adjustable shading
- Privacy: translucent materials
- Heat management: reflective coatings
- Seasonal changes: sutomated systems

Artificial Lighting Layers

Professional lighting design incorporates multiple layers to create appropriate illumination for different activities and times of day.

Ambient Lighting:

General illumination should provide comfortable base light levels:

- Living areas: 20-40 foot candles
- Kitchens: 30-50 foot candles
- Bathrooms: 40-60 foot candles
- Home offices: 50-70 foot candles
- Storage areas: 15-30 foot candles

Task Lighting:

Specific activities require appropriate illumination:

- Reading: 50-75 foot candles
- Cooking: 70-100 foot candles
- Grooming: 60-80 foot candles
- Crafts: 80-100 foot candles
- Detailed Work: 100-150 foot candles

Technology Integration

Modern lighting control systems offer sophisticated management options that enhance functionality and efficiency.

Control Systems:

Different situations benefit from varying control types:

- Occupancy Detection: Auto-activation
- Daylight Sensing: Light level adjustment
- Scene Programming: Activity-based settings
- Timer Functions: Schedule-based control
- Mobile Access: Remote management

Energy Management:

- Efficient lighting requires careful planning:
- LED Selection: Appropriate color temperatures
- Motion Sensors: Automatic deactivation
- Dimming Systems: Power reduction
- Daylight Harvesting: Natural light utilization
- Smart Controls: Usage optimization

IMPLEMENTATION GUIDELINES

Successful lighting implementation requires attention to both technical details and aesthetic considerations.

Installation Specifications:

- Fixture Mounting Heights
- Beam Spread Calculations
- Circuit Loading
- Control Zoning
- Emergency Lighting

Maintenance Planning:

Regular upkeep ensures optimal performance:

- Bulb Replacement Schedules
- Sensor Calibration
- Control Programming
- Fixture Cleaning
- System Updates

CHAPTER 11

SMART HOME TECHNOLOGY INTEGRATION

Smart Appliance Systems

Premium Smart Appliances:

1. Kitchen Integration

- Smart Refrigerators
- Samsung Family Hub ($3,000-7,000)
- Internal cameras
- Food management
- Family communication
- Entertainment options
- -LG InstaView ($2,500-6,000)
- Knock-twice viewing
- Smart ThinQ integration
- Energy monitoring
- Connected Cooking
- Smart Ranges
- GE Profile ($2,000-4,000)
- Remote monitoring

- Voice control
- Recipe integration
- Samsung Smart Range ($2,500-5,000)
- AI cooking assistance
- Remote temperature control
- Mobile notifications

2. Laundry Systems
- Smart Washers/Dryers
- LG ThinQ Series ($1,200-2,000 each)
- Remote start/monitoring
- Load optimization
- Energy usage tracking
- Samsung Smart Care ($1,000-1,800 each)
- Diagnostic systems
- Cycle customization
- Mobile notifications

Advanced HVAC Systems
1. Multi-Zone Mini-Split Systems
- Top Manufacturers:
- Mitsubishi
- Hyper-Heat Series ($4,000-8,000 per zone)
- Down to -13°F operation
- Smart control integration
- Individual zone control
- Daikin
- Multi-Zone System ($3,500-7,000 per zone)
- Energy monitoring
- Smart scheduling
- Voice control compatible
- LG
- Art Cool Series ($3,000-6,000 per zone)
- Designer aesthetics
- Ultra-quiet operation
- Smart ThinQ integration

2. Zone Control Technologies
- Smart Sensors:
- Temperature Monitoring
- Ecobee Room Sensors ($79 each)
- Motion detection
- Temperature averaging
- Occupancy learning
- Humidity Control
- Airthings Wave Plus ($229)
- Air quality monitoring
- Radon detection
- Data logging

Smart Lighting Integration
1. Advanced Control Systems
- Lutron Caseta ($80-100 per switch)
- Wireless dimming
- Scene control
- Smart home integration
- Away mode simulation
- Phillips Hue ($200-500 starter kit)
- Color changing
- Scene programming
- Entertainment integration
- Natural wake lighting

2. Automated Shading
- Lutron Serena ($500-1,000 per window)
- Solar tracking
- Schedule-based operation
- Energy optimization
- Smart home integration

CHAPTER 12

SUSTAINABLE ENERGY SYSTEMS

Tesla Powerwall Integration

1. Powerwall 3 System

Basic Specifications:

- Energy capacity: 13.5 kWh
- Power output: Up to 11.5 kW
- Dimensions: 62" x 26" x 6"
- Weight: approximately 343 lbs
- Installation requirements:
- Gateway installation
- Backup panel integration
- Internet connectivity
- Temperature-controlled location
- Professional installation
- Cost considerations:
- Hardware: $8,700-11,500
- Installation: $2,000-4,000
- Gateway: included
- Permits: varies by location

2. Solar Integration

System Components:

- Solar panels
- Premium options:
- Sunpower ($3.00-3.50 per watt)
- LG ($2.80-3.30 per watt)
- REC ($2.70-3.20 per watt)
- Inverter systems
- Microinverters:
- Enphase ($600-800 each)
- String inverters:
- Solaredge ($1,500-2,500)

Powerwall 3 with Gateway 3
Whole Home Backup

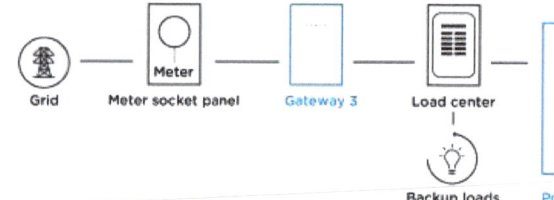

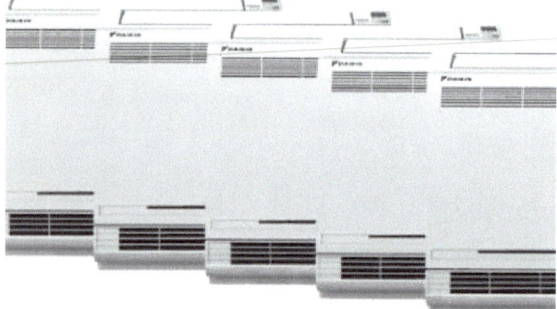

Powerwall 3 with Backup Switch
Whole Home Backup

Powerwall 3 with Backup Gateway 2
Partial Home Backup

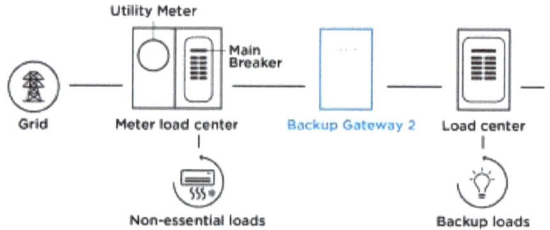

FLOOR HEATING SYSTEMS

1. Electric Systems

- Warmly ($12-20 per square foot)
- Ultra-thin mats
- Smart controls
- Zone management
- Schluter DITRA-HEAT ($15-25 per square foot)
- Integrated uncoupling
- Smart thermostat compatible
- Individual zone control

2. Hydronic Systems

- Viega ($18-25 per square foot)
- Energy efficient
- Even heat distribution
- Smart integration
- Uponor ($15-22 per square foot)
- Flow management
- Temperature control
- Zone optimization

INTEGRATION AND CONTROL

1. Central Management Systems

- Home Energy Management
- Tesla app
- Solar monitoring
- Powerwall control
- Energy usage tracking
- Storm watch features
- Third-party integration
- Home Assistant ($0-200)
- Samsung smartthings ($70-300)
- Apple homekit (varies)

2. Energy Monitoring

- Consumption tracking
- Sense energy monitor ($299)
- Real-time monitoring
- Device identification
- Usage patterns

- Cost tracking
- Emporia Vue ($149)
- Circuit-level monitoring
- Solar integration
- Mobile Alerts
- Energy reporting

THE VALUE OF SMART HOME TECHNOLOGY

Why Invest in Smart Technology?

Modern smart home technology represents more than convenience. It offers substantial efficiency, sustainability, and long-term benefits. Understanding these advantages helps justify the initial investment while ensuring lasting benefits for homeowners and the environment.

KEY BENEFITS OVERVIEW

1. Energy Efficiency
- 20-30% reduction in energy costs through smart HVAC systems
- 25-35% lighting energy savings with automated controls
- 10-15% appliance efficiency improvement with smart management
- Real-time usage monitoring for optimization
- Automatic adjustment to usage patterns

2. Enhanced Comfort and Convenience
- Precise temperature control in every room
- Automated lighting adjustment throughout the day
- Remote monitoring and control capabilities
- Predictive maintenance alerts
- Simplified home management

3. Long-term Value
- Increased property value (3-5% average)
- Reduced maintenance costs
- Extended system longevity
- Future-ready infrastructure
- Improved resale appeal

RECOMMENDED SYSTEMS AND BENEFITS

1. Mini-Split HVAC Systems
- Why Choose This Technology:
- 30-40% more efficient than traditional systems
- Individual zone control reduces wasted energy
- Quiet operation (as low as 19 decibels)
- No ductwork required
- Year-round comfort optimization

2. Tesla Powerwall and Solar Integration
- Key Advantages:
- Energy independence
- Backup power security
- Reduced carbon footprint
- Lower utility costs
- Storm protection features
- Smart grid integration

3. Smart Appliances

- Value Proposition:
- 15-20% energy savings
- Predictive maintenance
- Remote troubleshooting
- Improved functionality
- Extended lifespan through optimal operation

RECOVERY DIRECTORY

Manufacturers and Suppliers

1. HVAC Systems

- Mitsubishi Electric
  Website: www.mitsubishicomfort.com
  Product Info: Diamond Contractor network
  Training: Professional certification programs
- Daikin Website: www.daikincomfort.com
  Resources: Dealer locator, specification tools
  Support: Technical documentation

2. Energy Storage

- Tesla: Website: www.tesla.com/powerwall
  Support: Certified installer network
  Resources: Energy calculator, design tools
- LG Energy Solution
  Website: www.lgessbattery.com
  Products: Home battery solutions
  Support: Technical specifications

3. Smart Appliances

- Samsung
  Website: www.samsung.com/smart-home
  Support: SmartThings integration guides
  Resources: Product compatibility tools
- LG Website: www.lg.com/thinq
  Support: ThinQ technology guides
  Resources: Installation specifications

PROFESSIONAL ORGANIZATIONS

1. Smart Home Resources

- Consumer Technology Association
  Website: www.cta.tech
  Standards: Industry guidelines
  Training: Certification programs
- Home Technology Association
  Website: www.htacertified.org
  Certification: Professional standards
  Resources: Contractor selection guides

2. Energy Efficiency

- Energy Star
  Website: www.energystar.gov
  Tools: Product selection guides
  Resources: Savings calculators
- Department of Energy
  Website: www.energy.gov
  Resources: Energy efficiency guides
  Tools: Cost analysis calculators

INSTALLATION AND SUPPORT

1. Certified Installers

- Tesla Certified Installers
  Directory: www.tesla.com/support/certified-installers
  Requirements: Professional certification
  Training: Installation standards
- HVAC Excellence
  Website: www.hvacexcellence.org
  Certification: Professional standards
  Resources: Technical training

2. Technical Support

Smart Home Forums
Home Assistant Community
Professional Networks

CEDIA: www.cedia.net

CSA Group: www.csagroup.org

ASHRAE: www.ashrae.org

SUSTAINABILITY REASOURCES

1. Green Building

- USGBC

    Website: www.usgbc.org

    Resources: LEED certification

    Tools: Sustainability guidelines

- Energy.gov

    Website: www.energy.gov/energysaver

    Resources: Energy efficiency guides

    Tools: Savings calculators

2. Renewable Energy

- Solar Energy Industries Association

    Website: www.seia.org

    Resources: Solar installation guides

    Tools: Cost calculators

- Clean Energy States Alliance

    Website: www.cesa.org

    Resources: State incentive programs

    Tools: Policy guidelines

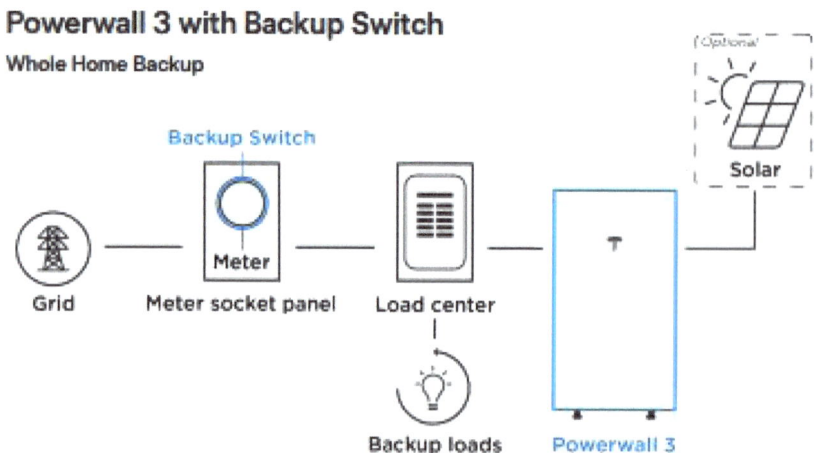

CHAPTER

13

CREATING HEALTHY INDOOR ENVIRONMENTS

A healthy home environment extends beyond aesthetics, including air quality, material safety, and overall wellness support. Modern homes should promote physical and psychological well-being through thoughtful design and material choices.

AIR QUALITY MANAGEMENT

Indoor Air Systems:

1. Ventilation Solutions

- Energy Recovery Ventilators (ERV)
  Cost: $1,500-4,000
- **Benefits:**

70-80% energy recovery

Humidity control

Pollutant removal

Fresh air exchange

Air Purification

Advanced HEPA Systems

Captures 99.97% of particles

VOC removal

Bacterial filtration

Smart monitoring Cost: $500-2,000

2. Humidity Control

  Whole-House Systems
  Cost: $2,000-4,000
- Features:
- Multi-zone control
- Smart monitoring
- Automatic adjustment
- Mold Prevention

MATERIAL SAFETY

Non-Toxic Materials:

1. Zero-VOC Finishes

- Paint Options
- Benjamin Moore Natura
- Material Safety
- Sherwin-Williams Harmony
- ECOS Paints
- Cost: $45-75/gallon

2. Safe Flooring Choices

- Solid Hardwood
- Natural Linoleum
- Cork Flooring
- Wool Carpet
- Cost: $8-20/sq ft

WELLNESS FEATURES

1. Circadian Lighting

- Smart LED Systems
- Wellness Features
- Color temperature control
- Natural light simulation
- Automated adjustment
- Energy efficient
- Cost: $200-500/room

2. Sound Management

- Acoustic Treatments
- Sound absorption panels
- Noise reduction materials
- Vibration control
- Cost: $5-15/sq ft

CHAPTER 14

PURPOSE-DRIVEN STORAGE SOLUTIONS

Effective storage design focuses on accessibility, functionality, and space optimization. Professional storage solutions should enhance daily living while maintaining aesthetic appeal.

KITCHEN STORAGE SYSTEM

1. Cabinet Organization
- Premium Solutions:
- Pull-out Systems
- Blum LEGRABOX
- Full extension
- Soft close
- Weight capacity: 88 lbs
- Cost: $200-400/drawer
- Corner Solutions
- LeMans II System
- Full access
- Smooth operation
- Weight capacity: 65 lbs
- Cost: $400-800/unit

2. Pantry Organization
- Roll-out Systems
- Features:
- Adjustable shelving
- Full extension
- Custom width options
- Cost: $300-700/unit

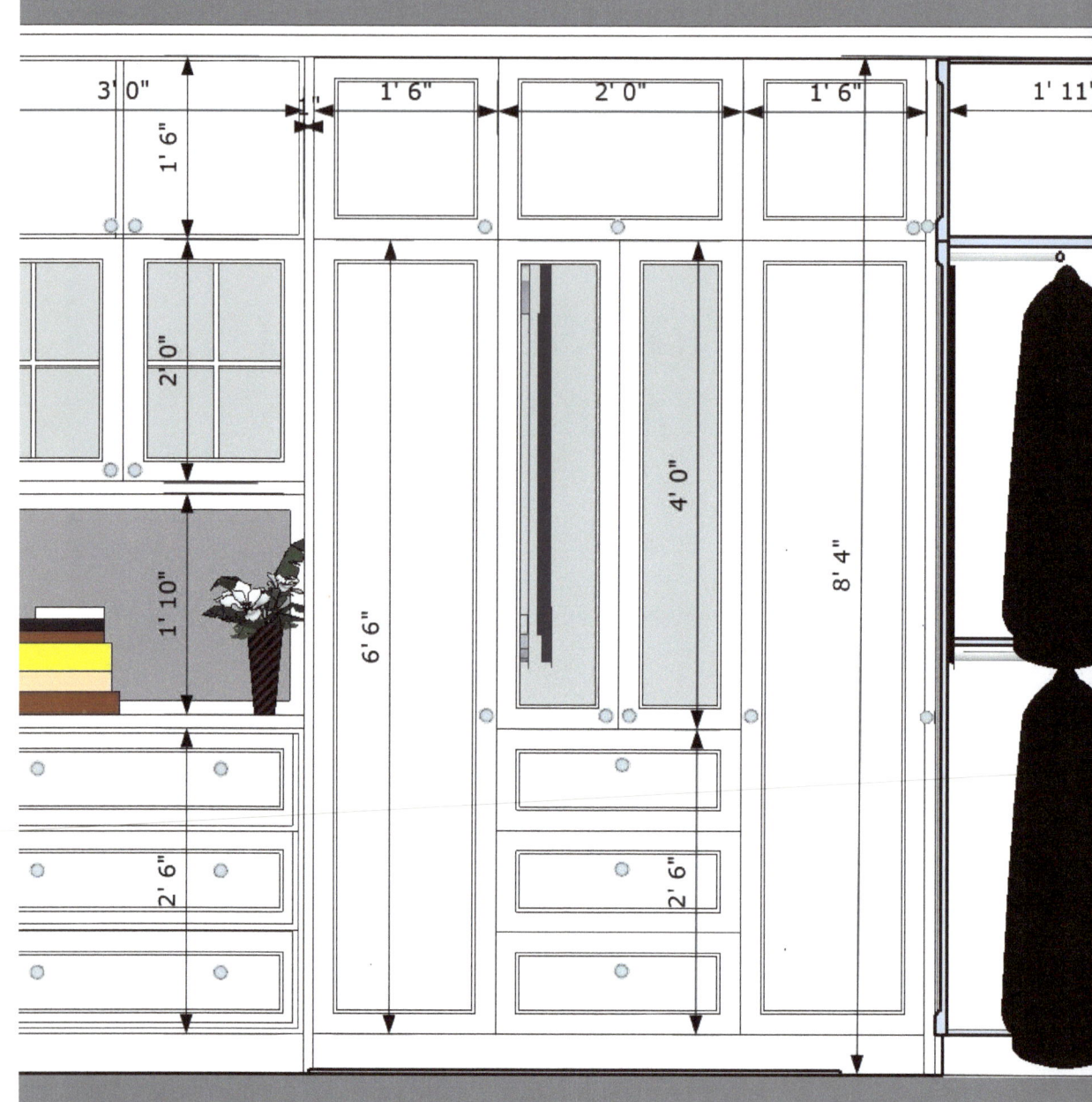

CLOSET SYSTEMS

1. Custom Solutions

Premium Options:
California Closets
Custom design
Professional installation
Lifetime warranty

cost: $150-300/linear ft
Organized Living
Modular systems
DIY installation option
10-year warranty
Cost: $100-200/linear ft

2. Specialty Storage

Shoe Organization
Rotating systems
Pull-out racks
Custom shelving
Cost: $200-500/unit
Accessory Storage
Jewelry drawers

Belt/tie racks
Valet rods
Cost: $50-200/component

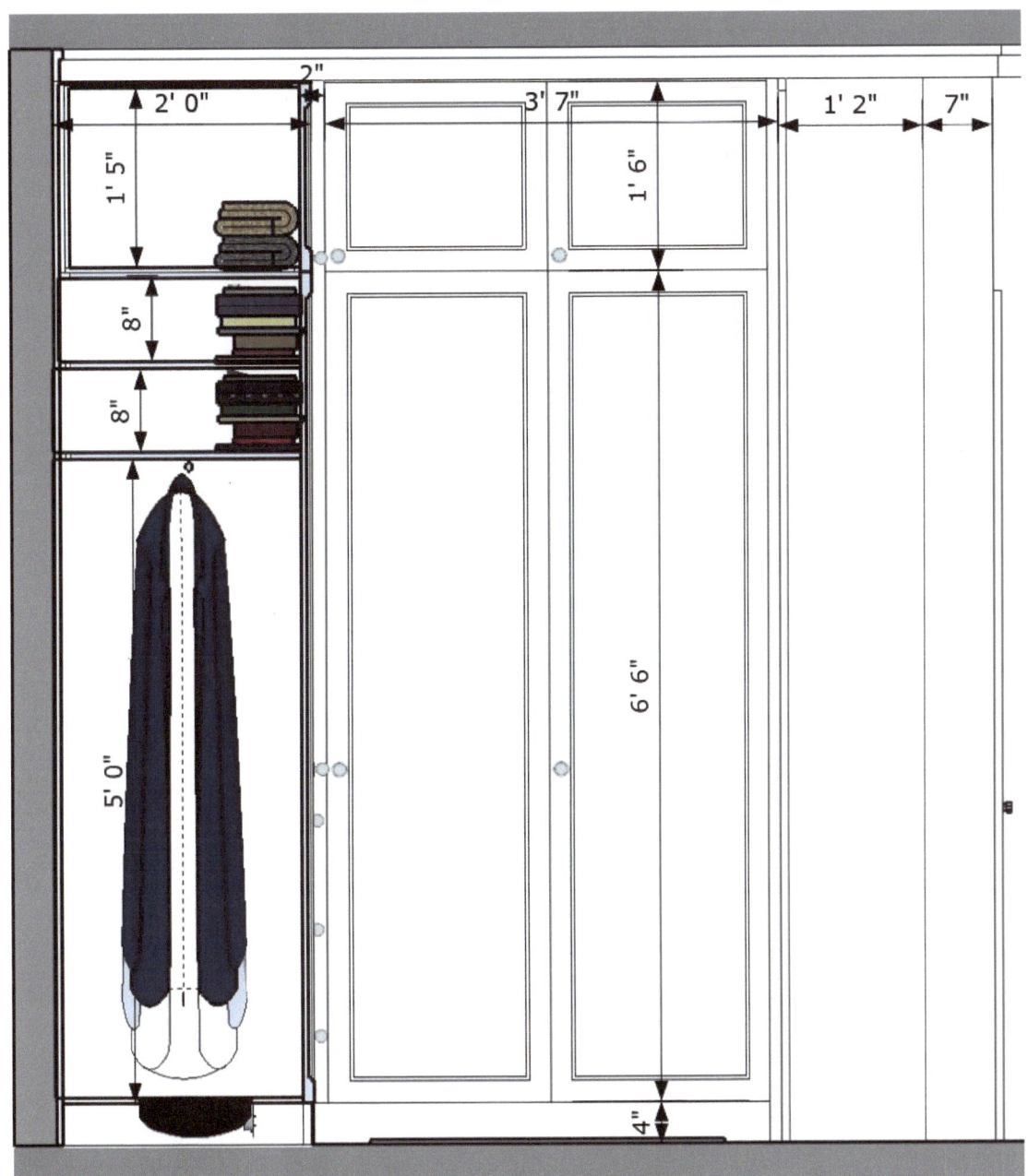

MULTI-FUNCTINAL SOLUTION

1. Built-in Features

Window Seats
Multi-functional Solutions
Storage integration
Custom cushions
Ventilation planning

Cost: $1,500-3,000/unit
Under-stair Storage
Pull-out drawers
Access doors
Custom shelving
Cost: $2,000-5,000/system

2. Furniture Solutions

Ottoman Storage
High-quality hinges
Safety stops
Fabric options
Cost: $300-800/piece
Bed Storage

Hydraulic lift systems
Side drawers
Headboard storage
Cost: $1,000-3,000/unit

IMPLEMENTATION GUIDELINES

Storage Planning Process:

1. Needs Assessment
- Item inventory
- Usage patterns
- Access requirements
- Growth projections

2. Design Development
- Space utilization
- Material selection
- Hardware choices
- Installation planning

3. Installation Sequence
- Preparation work
- System installation
- Hardware mounting
- Final adjustments

MAINTENANCE REQUIREMENTS

1. Regular Care:
- Hardware Inspection
- Monthly checks
- Lubrication schedule
- Adjustment needs
- Replacement planning

2. System Updates
- Annual evaluation
- Component updates
- Organization review
- Capacity assessment

CHAPTER

15

FUTURE-PROOFING YOUR HOME

Creating a home that remains functional and valuable over time requires thoughtful planning and strategic implementation. Future-proofing considers technological advancement and lifestyle changes while maintaining flexibility for evolving needs.

INFRASTRUCTURE PLANNING

1. Electrical Systems

- Smart infrastructure:

High-Capacity Panels

200-400 amp service

Smart monitoring capability

EV charging readiness

Solar integration preparation

Cost: $2,500-6,000

- Wiring infrastructure

Conduit systems for future runs

Data cable pathways

Multiple circuit availability

Surge protection

Cost: $3-5 per square foot

2. Network Infrastructure

- Data systems:
- Structured wiring
- CAT6A or CAT7 cabling
- Fiber optic preparation
- Multiple access points
- Security integration
- Cost: $4-7 per square foot

ADAPTABLE DESIGN ELEMENTS

1. Flexible Spaces

- Multi-purpose rooms:
- Modular design
- Moveable walls
- Adaptable lighting
- Variable power locations
- Sound management
- Cost: $100-200 per square foot
- Smart Storage
- Reconfigurable systems
- Technology integration
- Hidden infrastructure
- Easy modification
- Cost: $75-150 per linear foot

2. Universal Design Features

- Accessibility Considerations:
- Wide doorways (36" minimum)
- Zero-threshold entries
- Reinforced bathroom walls
- Adjustable counter heights
- Cost: 5-10% of renovation budget

TECHNOLOGY INTEGRATION

1. Smart Home Foundation

- Core Systems:
- Central Hub
- Professional-grade processor
- Multiple protocol support
- Remote access security
- Expandable architecture
- Cost: $2,000-5,000
- Device integration
- Matter protocol ready
- Thread network support
- WiFi 6E compatibility
- Bluetooth 5.0+
- Cost: Varies by device

2. Energy Management

- Future systems:
- Solar readiness
- Roof preparation
- Electrical integration
- Battery storage planning
- Grid connection
- Cost: $5,000-10,000

- preparation
- Energy storage
- Battery space allocation
- Inverter location planning
- Cooling system preparation
- Monitoring integration
- Cost: $3,000-7,000 preparation

LONG TERM VALUE CONSIDERATION

1. Material Selection

- Sustainable Choices:
- Durable Flooring
- 50+ year lifespan materials
- Easy repair options
- Style longevity
- Low maintenance
- Cost premium: 20-30%
- Quality Fixtures
- Timeless designs
- Replaceable parts
- Strong warranties
- Brand longevity
- Cost Premium: 30-40%

2. System Upgradability

- Future-ready design:
- Modular components
- Easy replacement
- Technology updates
- Part availability
- Backward compatibility
- Cost Premium: 15-25%
- Priority planning

IMPLEMENTATION STRATEGY

1. Phase Implementation:

- Essential infrastructure
- Electrical backbone
- Network foundation
- Structural preparation
- HVAC readiness
- Timeline: Initial phase
- Adaptable elements
- Flexible spaces
- Modular systems
- Technology integration
- Storage solutions
- Timeline: secondary phase

2. Budget Allocation

- Investment Strategy:
- Core Infrastructure: 40%
- Adaptable Systems: 30%
- Technology Integration: 20%
- Future Planning: 10%

REASOURCE DIRECTORY

1. Professional Organizations

- Planning resources:
- American institute of Architects
- Future-proofing guidelines
- Design standards
- Professional network
- CEDIA
- Technology integration
- Best practices
- Certified professionals

2. Product Sources

- Recommended Suppliers:
- Infrastructure Components
- egrand
- Lutron
- Cisco
- Ubiquiti
- Adaptable Systems
- Häfele
- Blum
- Spaceworks
- Transform
- Technology Partners
- Integration Specialists:
- Control Systems
- Control4
- Crestron
- Savant
- RTI
- Energy Management
- Tesla
- Enphase
- SolarEdge
- Generac

APPENDIX A: COMPARISON CHARTS AND BUYING GUIDES

Furniture Buying Guide

Price Point Comparison Chart

Brand	Price range	Best known for	Lead time	Customization options	Warranty
Rove concepts	$$$$	Modern Luxury, Premium Materials	8-12 weeks	High	10 years
Blu Dot	$$$	Contemporary design, Quality Craftmanship	2-4 weeks	Limited	10 years
CB2	$$$	Modern Style, Trending Designs	1-8 weeks	Moderate	1 year
Modani	$$$	Europian Inspired Modern	1-4 weeks	Limited	10 years
Hause	$$$$	Designers collaborations	8-12 weeks	Limited	1 year
Castlery	$$	Value Modern Furniture	2-4 weeks	Limited	Lifetime
Homary	$$	Diverse Styles, Modern Luxury	2-6 weeks	Moderate	1 year

Best Times to Buy Furniture

- January: Post-holiday clearance
- February: Presidents' Day sales
- May: Memorial Day sales
- July: Independence Day sales, outdoor furniture clearance
- September: Labor Day sales
- November: Black Friday/Cyber Monday
- December: Year-end clearance

Appliance Comparison Guide

Luxury Range Comparison

Brand	Price range	Signature Features	Warranty	Made in	BTU Range
Viking	$$$$	Professional performance, Custom color	Limited, Lifetime	USA	15K-23K
Sub-Zero	$$$$$	Dual Refrigeration, Air Purification	2-12 years	USA	N/A
Hestan	$$$$$	CircuFlame™ burners, Custom colors	Limited, Lifetime	USA	23K-30K
Bertazzoni	$$$$	Italian Designs, Color options	2 years	Italy	15K-19K
Miele	$$$$$	MrChef Programs, Precision	1-2 years	Germany	12K-19K

Mid-Range Appliance Features

Brand	Smart Features	Energy Star	Wi-Fi	Voice Control	App Control
Bosch	✓✓✓	✓✓✓✓	✓✓✓	✓✓	✓✓✓
Z Line	✓✓	✓✓✓	✓✓	✓	✓✓
Fomo	✓✓	✓✓✓	✓✓	✓	✓✓
Thor	✓✓	✓✓✓	✓	✓	✓
Electrolux	✓✓✓	✓✓✓	✓✓✓	✓✓	✓✓✓
LG	✓✓✓✓	✓✓✓✓	✓✓✓	✓✓✓	✓✓✓✓

AI and Digital Tools Comparision

Design Visualization Tools

Tool	Best For	Learning Curve	Price Range	Key Features	Output Format
Midjourney	Concept Visualization	Moderate	$$$$	AI Powered, Highly Detailed	Images
Apply Design	Space Planning	Easy	$$	Room layout Planning, 3D Rendering	3D/2D Plans
SketchUp	3D Modeling	High	$$-$$$$	Professional Tools	3D Models
Planner 5D	Quick Layouts	Easy	$-$$	User Friendly, Mobile	2D/3D Plans
Room Sketcher	Floor Plans	Moderate	$$-$$$	Professional Features	2D/3D Plans

Material Selection Guide

Countertop Comparison

Material	Price Range	Durability	Maintenance	Eco-Friendly	Heat Resistance
Quartz	$$$-$$$$	✓✓✓✓	Easy	✓✓✓	✓✓✓✓
Granite	$$$-$$$$	✓✓✓	Moderate	✓✓	✓✓✓✓✓
Marble	$$$$-$$$$	✓✓	High	✓✓	✓✓✓
Butcher Block	$$-$$$	✓✓	High	✓✓✓✓	✓✓
Concrete	$$-$$$	✓✓✓	Moderate	✓✓✓	✓✓✓

Flooring Options

Type	Cost/sqft	Durability	Water Resistante	Installation Difficulty	Lifespan
Hardwood	$$$-$$$$	✓✓✓	✓✓	High	25+ Years
LVP	$$-$$$	✓✓✓	✓✓✓✓✓	Easy	10-20 Years
Tile	$$-$$$$	✓✓✓✓✓	✓✓✓✓	High	50+ Years
Engineered Wood	$$-$$$	✓✓✓	✓✓✓	Moderate	15-30 YEARS
Laminate	$-$$	✓✓✓	✓✓	Easy	10-15 Years

PROJECT PLANNING TEMPLATE

- Budget Allocation Guide
- Design and Planning: 5-10%
- Construction Labor: 30-35%
- Materials: 30-40%
- Appliances and Fixtures: 10-20%
- Furniture and Decor: 5-15%
- Contingency: 10-20%

TIMELINE PLANNING GUIDE

1. Planning Phase: 1-2 months

- Design development
- Contractor selection
- Permitting

2. Demolition: 1-2 weeks

3. Construction Phase: 2-6 months

- Rough-in work
- Installations
- Finishing work

4. Final Phase: 2-4 weeks

- Punch list
- Cleaning
- Decorating

QUALITY CONTROL CHECKLIST

- Pre-construction documentation
- Daily progress photos
- Material verification
- Installation inspection points
- Final walkthrough criteria
- Warranty documentation requirements

CHAPTER 16

CURATED SHOPPING RESOURCES

The success of any home design project relies heavily on the quality of materials and products selected. Through years of professional experience, I have carefully curated this collection of trusted resources. Each supplier has been chosen for their consistent quality, reliable service, and excellent value proposition.

Premium furniture Retailers

- **Modern Design Leaders**
- **Rove Concepts** (www.roveconcepts.com)

This Vancouver-based company specializes in modern and contemporary furniture that combines sophistication with comfort. Their pieces feature clean lines, premium materials, and exceptional craftsmanship. Its member program sets it apart, which provides significant savings and early access to new collections. Their in-house designs often draw inspiration from mid-century modern classics while incorporating contemporary elements.

CB2 (www.cb2.com)

As Crate & Barrels modern furnishing division, CB2 offers sophisticated contemporary pieces at affordable prices. Their furniture combines style with practicality, and frequently collaborates with notable designers to create exclusive collections. Their quality control standards are particularly impressive for their price range, and they offer excellent customer service.

Blu Dot (www.bludot.com)

Known for their innovative approach to modern design, Blu Dot creates original pieces that balance form and function. Their furniture often incorporates clever design solutions while maintaining clean aesthetics. Their commitment to quality is evident in their attention to detail and excellent warranty service.

STYLE-FORWARD OPTIONS

Homary (www.homary.com)

This retailer offers a wide range of contemporary and modern furniture at competitive prices. Their selection includes everything from statement pieces to practical everyday furniture. They excel in offering trend-forward designs while maintaining quality standards.

Castlery (www.castlery.com/us)

Specializing in modern furniture that combines style with value, Castlery offers well-designed pieces at reasonable prices. Their direct-to-consumer model allows them to maintain quality while keeping prices accessible. They are particularly known for their comfortable seating options and dining collections.

Modani (www.modani.com)

This retailer focuses on modern and contemporary furniture with a European influence. Their pieces often feature bold designs while maintaining functionality. They offer good value for money, especially in their living room and bedroom collections.

Luxury and Specialty Retailers
Global Views (www.globalviews.com)

Offering high-end decorative accessories and furniture, Global Views is known for its unique designs and exceptional quality. Their pieces often serve as stunning focal points in well-designed spaces. They're particularly strong in accessories and accent furniture.

Burke Decor (www.burkedecor.com)

This curator of fine home furnishings offers a carefully selected range of furniture and decor. They excel in offering unique pieces that can define a space. Their customer service is notably professional, and they offer excellent design guidance.

Perigold (www.perigold.com)

As Wayfairs luxury division, Perigold provides access to high-end brands and designer collections.

They offer an extensive selection of premium furniture and decor, with excellent customer service and white-glove delivery options.

Arhaus (arhaus.com)

Arhaus are Known for its artisanal furniture-making approach, Arhaus creates pieces that blend traditional craftsmanship with contemporary design. Their furniture showcases excellent build quality and distinctive styling.

PREMIUM MATTRESS SELECTION

Somnus Haven (www.somnushaven.com)

This specialized online retailer offers a carefully curated selection of premium and organic mattresses, along with sustainable luxury bedding. Their focus on quality sleep solutions includes environmentally conscious options and exceptional customer service. They excel in providing detailed product information and expert guidance for selecting the ideal sleep system.

Fuse Specialty Appliances (www.fusespecialtyappliances.com)

Known for its curated selection of premium appliances, Fuse focuses on innovative, high-performance products. They offer excellent technical knowledge and support throughout the selection and installation process.

Luwa Luxury (www.luwaluxury.com)

This retailer focuses on luxury appliances and offers exceptional service. They excel in providing comprehensive solutions for high-end kitchens and maintaining strong relationships with premium manufacturers.

Bertazzoni (us.bertazzoni.com)

This renowned Italian manufacturer combines engineering excellence with elegant design. Their appliances feature exceptional build quality and innovative cooking technology. Each piece reflects six generations of family expertise in kitchen appliance manufacturing, offering both professional performance and sophisticated aesthetics.

Marcelin (marcelin.com)

Specializing in premium appliance selections, Marcelin offers comprehensive kitchen solutions. Their extensive product knowledge and exceptional customer service simplify complex appliance decisions, ensuring optimal selections for each project.

Z-Line Kitchen (zlinekitchen.com)

Known for its professional-grade range hoods and cooking appliances, Z-Line offers excellent value in the premium segment. Its products combine commercial-grade performance with a refined design, making them ideal for residential use.

Kitchen Cabinetry Cabinet Set (binetset.com)

Offering a wide range of cabinet styles and finishes, Cabinet Set provides excellent value without compromising on quality. Their online design tools and professional support help ensure successful outcomes for any kitchen project

Eat Gather Love (eatgatherlove.com)

This boutique cabinet manufacturer specializes in custom solutions combining functionality and elegant design. Their attention to detail and quality craftsmanship suit them for high-end kitchen renovations.

Counntertop Materials (cosentino.com/usa)

Cosentino demonstrates excellence in engineered stone surfaces through their Dekton and Silestone products.Their manufacturing processes create exceptionally durable surfaces that resist scratching, staining, and heat damage. Their commitment to innovation has produced unique aesthetics and performance characteristics that set new standards in the industry.

Butcher Block Co. (hardwood-lumber.com)

Specializes in premium wood surfaces, combining natural beauty and functional durability. Their products feature carefully selected hardwoods and expert craftsmanship, with particular attention to food safety and maintenance requirements. Their educational resources provide valuable guidance for product selection and care.

Country Mouldings (www.countrymouldings.com)

Excels in providing specialized wood surfaces and custom millwork solutions. Their attention to detail and quality craftsmanship ensure exceptional results for custom projects. Their products feature premium materials and expert construction techniques, maintaining stability and appearance over time.

Cambri (www.cambriausa.com)

Leading manufacturer of premium quartz surfaces, Cambria offers exceptional durability and stunning designs. Their American-made products feature groundbreaking patterns and superior engineering.

PaperStone Products (paperstoneproducts.com)

This innovative company produces sustainable countertops from recycled paper and non-petroleum resin. Their products offer excellent durability while maintaining strong environmental credentials.

IceStone USA (icestoneusa.com)

Specializing in recycled glass surfaces, IceStone creates unique, sustainable countertops that combine environmental responsibility with striki-ing aesthetics.

Cabinet Hardware Solutions

Residence Supply (**residencesupply.com**) It is a comprehensive hardware resource, offering an expertly curated selection of architectural hardware. Their collection ranges from contemporary to traditional styles, emphasizing quality craftsmanship and durability. Detailed product specifications and excellent customer service make complex hardware decisions straightforward..

Build.com

Build (**build.com/cabinet-hardware**) is a leading online hardware retailer that offers an extensive selection of cabinet hardware and architectural accessories. Their user-friendly website provides detailed product information, installation guides, and competitive pricing, ensuring options for every style and budget.

Fine Knobs (fineknobs.com)

Fine Knobs Specializing in premium cabinet hardware, Fine Knobs offers distinctive pieces that can transform ordinary cabinetry into extraordinary features. Their carefully selected collection includes both classic and contemporary designs, with exceptional attention to finish quality and durability.

Signature Hardware (signaturehardware.com)

Known for its comprehensive selection of premium hardware and fixtures, it combines quality with a distinctive design. Their product range spans traditional to contemporary styles, with excellent customer service and product support.

FLOORING AND WALL

Tile Club (tileclub.com)

This curated tile source offers designer-quality selections at competitive prices. Their collection ranges from classic to contemporary, with excellent quality control and customer service.

Florida Design Works (floridadesignworks.com)

Providing comprehensive flooring solutions, this supplier offers exceptional variety and technical expertise. Their professional support ensures appropriate material selection for specific applications.

COREtec (coretecfloors.com)

Innovators in luxury vinyl flooring, COREtec products offer excellent durability and water resistance while maintaining sophisticated aesthetics.

Tile Bar (tilebar.com)

Known for their designer-quality tile selections, it offers innovative patterns and materials. Their collection features exclusive designs and excellent quality control, with professional support for complex installations.

Panel Town (paneltown.com)

This specialist in architectural panels provides innovative wall and ceiling solutions. Their products combine aesthetic appeal with practical functionality, making them suitable for both residential and commercial applications.

The Tile Shop (tileshop.com)

Offers a comprehensive selection of tile and stone products. The Tile Shop combines quality materials with excellent customer service. Their showrooms and design services help ensure successful project outcomes.

WALL COVERING AND ARCHITECTURAL SURFACES

Luxe Wall (luxewall.com)

Specializing in premium wall treatments, Luxe Wall offers innovative solutions for creating distinctive interior spaces. Their products combine visual impact with practical durability.

Phillip Jeffries (phillipjeffries.com)

Phillip Jeffries, the industry leader in natural, textured, and specialty wallcoverings, offers exceptional quality and design sophistication. Their natural materials and artisanal techniques create unique wall finishes.

Graham & Brown (grahambrown.com/us)

Combining traditional expertise with contemporary design, Graham & Brown offers innovative wallcoverings that range from classic to cutting-edge. Their products feature excellent quality and installation-friendly properties.

Vant Panels (vantpanels.com)

Vant Panels Specializes in innovative wall panels and headboards, and Vant Panels offers customizable solutions for creating distinctive wall features. Their products combine modern design with practical installation systems.

The Wood Veneer Hub

The Wood Veneer Hub **(thewoodveneerhub.**

com) This specialized supplier of wood veneers provides high-quality materials for custom wall treatments. Their extensive selection includes common and exotic species, with excellent technical support.

ATI Laminates (atilaminates.com)

Offers innovative laminate solutions that combine durability with distinctive design. Their products include both standard and custom options, suitable for various applications.

Wallism (wallism.com/us)

This contemporary wallcovering specialist offers innovative designs and materials. Their collection features unique patterns and textures with excellent quality and installation properties.

Limitless Walls (limitlesswalls.com)

Provides custom murals and coverings. Limitless Walls offers unique solutions for creating distinctive spaces. Their digital printing technology allows unlimited design possibilities while maintaining quality and durability.

Grasscloth and More (grassclothandmore.com)

Specializing in natural fibre wallcoverings, this supplier offers authentic materials with excellent visual and tactile qualities. Their collection includes traditional and contemporary interpretations of classic grass cloth lighting solutions.

Ozark Lighting (Ozarke.com)

Ozark Lighting specializes in distinctive fixtures that combine unique design with quality construction. Their collections range from contemporary to transitional styles, with a strong focus on material quality and finish durability. Their products undergo thorough testing for both electrical safety and mechanical stability.

Residence Supply's lighting collection highlights distinctive designs that serve as functional art pieces. Their selection process emphasizes both visual impact and practical functionality. Additionally, their customer service includes detailed technical support to assist with proper selection and installation considerations.

Burke Decor Lighting (burkedecor.com/collections/lighting)

Burke Decor offers carefully curated lighting selections and focuses on distinctive designs that serve as functional art pieces. Their collection ranges from contemporary to transitional styles.

BATHROOM FIXTURES AND ACCESSORIES

Mod Lighting (mod-lighting.com)

Specialists in modern lighting solutions; Mod Lighting combines innovative design with excellent functionality. Their fixtures feature quality construction and sophisticated styling. Each supplier has been selected based on consistent quality, service, and value performance. Their inclusion in this resource guide reflects years of professional experience and successful project implementations. When working with these suppliers, consider their specific strengths and specializations to ensure optimal results for your project requirements.

Lux Home (luxhome.co)

This premium bathroom fixture supplier offers sophisticated and refined solutions for modern bathrooms. Their collection features innovative designs with quality materials, and excellent craftsmanship. Their product range includes contemporary and traditional styles, focusing on lasting quality.

BrassNA (brassna.com)

Specializing in premium brass fixtures and accessories, Brass NA combines traditional craftsmanship with modern design. Their products feature exceptional build quality and distinctive finishes, making them ideal for luxury bathroom projects.

On Floating Vanity (onfloatingvanity.com)

This specialized retailer focuses on contemporary bathroom solutions, particularly wall-mounted vanities. Their products combine space-saving design with sophisticated aesthetics, perfect for modern bathroom renovations.

The Interior Gallery (theinteriorgallery.com)

Offering a comprehensive selection of bathroom fixtures and accessories, The Interior Gallery provides quality products across various style categories. Their curated collection emphasizes both functionality and aesthetic appeal.

The Bath Outlet (thebathoutlet.com)

This comprehensive bathroom resource offers quality fixtures and accessories at competitive prices. Their extensive product range includes everything from basic fixtures to luxury items, with excellent customer service and product support.

Vintage Tub (vintagetub.com)

Specializing in classic and vintage-style bathroom fixtures, Vintage Tub offers unique pieces that add character to bathroom designs. Their collection includes both authentic period pieces and quality reproductions.

QUALITY ASSESSMENT GUIDELINES

Material Quality Metrics

Surface Materials:
- Hardness Rating (Minimum Requirements)
- Flooring: 1000+ on the Janka scale for hardwoods
- Title: 7+ on the Mohs scale
- Stone: Grade A or equivalent
- Porcelain: Water absorption
- Finish Durability:
- UV Resistance: 1000+ hours without visible change
- Scratch Resistance: 7+ on Mohs scale for countertops
- Impact Resistance: Minimum 8 ft-lb impact without damage
- Chemical Resistance: No visible effect from common household chemicals

Construction Quality Indicators

Furniture Assessment:
- Frame Construction
- Hardwood or engineered wood construction
- Reinforced corners and stress points

- Proper wood moisture content (6-8%)
- Quality joinery methods Upholstery Standards:
- Fabric durability: 30,000+ double rubs
- Seam strength: 40+ pounds per inch
- Pattern matching at seams
- Professional-grade padding density

Price Comparision Tools
Cost Analysis Matrix
Kitchen Cabinetry Cost Comparison

Grade Level	Materials	Construction	Hardware	Finish	Price/Linear ft
Builder	MDF/Part	Stapled	Basic	Basic	$100-$200
Premium	Plywood	Doweled	Medium	Standard	$200-$400
Luxury	Hardwood	Dovetailed	Premium	Custom	$400-$800

Countertop Materia Comparison

Material	Durability	Maintenance	Aesthetics	Cost/sqFt
Quartz	Excellent	Low	High	$60-$100
Granite	Very Good	Medium	High	$40-$100
Solid Surface	Very Good	Low	Medium	$35-$80
Butcher Block	Good	High	High	$40-$100

VALUE ASSESSMENT TOOLS

Investment Priority Matrix:

- Essential Elements (40% of budget)
- Core infrastructure
- Primary surfaces
- Major fixtures
- Base cabinetry

Functional Upgrades (30% of budget)

- Storage solutions
- Lighting systems
- Appliance features
- Technology integration

Aesthetic Elements (20% of budget)

- Decorative features
- Finish upgrades
- Accent pieces
- Special materials

Contingency Reserve (10% of budget)

- Unexpected conditions
- Design modifications
- Material upgrades
- Installation adjustments

BUYING GUIDE FRAMEWORK

Material Selection Process

Step 1: Requirements Assessment

- Analyze usage patterns
- Evaluate environmental conditions
- Determine maintenance capacity
- Consider long-term durability needs

Step 2: Performance Evaluation

- Review technical specifications
- Assess maintenance requirements
- Compare warranty coverage
- Evaluate installation requirements

Step 3: Value Analysis

- Compare initial costs
- Calculate lifetime value
- Assess maintenance costs
- Consider replacement cycles

SHOPPING STRATEGY

1. Research Phase

Begin by exploring multiple retailers websites to understand their offerings and price ranges. Many offer design inspiration and room planning tools that can help visualize possibilities.

2. Sample Orders

Order material samples or visit showrooms to assess quality in person when possible. This is particularly important for upholstered furniture and finish materials.

3. Timing Purchases

Many of these retailers offer significant savings during specific sales periods. Consider timing non-urgent purchases to align with these opportunities.

4. Customer Service

Take advantage of the design assistance many of these retailers offer. Their expertise can help ensure selections will work well in your space.

Remember that quality furnishings and appliances are long-term investments. While initial costs might be higher than mass-market alternatives, the durability, functionality, and aesthetic longevity these selections offer typically provide better value over time.

CHAPTER
17

INTERIOR DESIGN AND RENOVATION MENTORSHIP PROGRAM

BRIDGING THEORY AND PRACTICE

Throughout my sixteen years in interior design and construction project management, we've observed that success in this field comes from understanding and applying principles in real-world situations. The gap between theory and practical application often presents the biggest challenge for professionals and enthusiasts. This observation has inspired the creation of a comprehensive mentorship program, launching in Fall 2025.

PROGRAM OVERVIEW

The Interior Design and Renovation Mentorship Program provides hands-on guidance and practical knowledge for individuals looking to enhance their understanding of design and renovation processes. Whether you're a practicing interior decorator seeking to expand your expertise, a homeowner planning a major renovation, or an Airbnb host wanting to maximize your property potential, this program offers tailored guidance to help, you achieve your goals.

WHO SHOULD PARTICIPATE

This program is specifically designed for:

Interior Decorators
- Expand your technical knowledge
- Learn project management skills
- Understand construction processes
- Develop contractor relationships
- Master budget management

Homeowners
- Navigate renovation processes
- Make informed design decisions
- Understand cost implications
- Manage contractors effectively
- Avoid common pitfalls

Trade Contractors
- Enhance design understanding
- Improve client communication
- Develop collaborative skills
- Expand service offerings
- Increase project value

Airbnb Hosts
- Maximize space functionality
- Create memorable environments
- Optimize durability
- Manage renovation timelines
- Balance aesthetics and practicality

Staging Designers
- Develop efficient systems
- Enhance property value
- Create immediate impact
- Manage resources effectively
- Build professional networks

Design Enthusiasts
- Gain practical knowledge
- Understand design principles
- Learn industry practices
- Develop professional skills
- Build confidence

PROGRAM STRUCTURE

The mentorship program combines various learning formats to ensure a comprehensive understanding and practical application:

Group Sessions
- Monthly virtual workshops
- Real project analysis
- Problem-solving exercises
- Industry expert guests
- Peer learning opportunities

Individual Guidance
- Project-specific advice
- Portfolio development
- Career planning
- Technical support

Practical Application
- Hands-on projects
- Material selection analysis
- Budget planning practice
- Timeline development

CORE CURRICULUM AREAS

The program covers essential aspects of design and renovation:

Design Development
- Style analysis and selection
- Space planning principles
- Material compatibility
- Color theory application
- Lighting design

Project Management
- Budget development
- Timeline creation
- Contractor coordination
- Quality control
- Problem resolution

Technical Knowledge
- Construction basics
- Material specifications
- Code requirements
- Installation methods
- Safety protocols

Business Practices
- Client communication
- Proposal development
- Contract management
- Documentation systems
- Professional networking

PROGRAM BENEFITS

- Participants will gain:
- Practical industry knowledge
- Professional connections
- Problem-solving skills
- Resource Access
- Ongoing support

ENROLLMENT INFORMATION

The inaugural session begins in the Fall 2025 with limited spots to ensure personalized attention. Early registration is recommended.

Contact Information

For program details and registration:
Email: tam@tam-interiors.com

Program Options
- Full mentorship program
- Specialized focus tracks
- Project-specific guidance
- Group learning opportunities

A PERSONAL NOTE

As I transition from active practice to mentoring, I'm thrilled to share the insights and expertise I've gained through years of hands-on experience. This program is more than just a transfer of knowledge, it's about fostering a community of informed, confident, and successful design professionals and enthusiasts.

My journey from refugee to accomplished design professional has reinforced the importance of both knowledge and real-world experience. This program blends both, offering you the opportunity to learn from practical scenarios while honing your skills.

I invite you to be part of this exciting educational journey. Whether you're looking to elevate your professional expertise, manage your own renovation project, or deepen your understanding of design and renovation, this program provides the guidance and support you need to succeed.

Let's connect and discuss how this program can help you achieve your goals. I look forward to walking this path with you and contributing to your success in the world of interior design and renovation.

Remember, great design isn't just about aesthetics—it's about creating spaces that enrich lives. Together, let's turn that vision into reality.

www.ingramcontent.com/pod-product-compliance
Lightning Source LLC
Chambersburg PA
CBHW041527220426
43670CB00003B/52